Cop*[barcode]*

The characters and events ... Any similarity
to real persons, living or de... by the author.

No part of this book may be reproduced, or stored in a retrieval system,
or transmitted in any form or by any means, electronic, mechanical,
photocopying, recording, or otherwise, without express written permission
of the publisher.

ISBN-13: 9798316638437
ISBN-10: 1477123456

Cover design by: Art Painter
Library of Congress Control Number: 2018675309
Printed in the United States of America

TABLE OF CONTENTS

Introduction

Chapter 1: The Many Faces of Loss: Understanding Different Types of Grief

Chapter 2: Recognising Grief Behaviours: Your Body's Response to Loss

Chapter 3: Navigating the Fog: Essential Tools for Mindful Mourning

Chapter 4: Breaking the Timeline: Permission to Grieve at Your Own Pace

Chapter 5: Sacred Spaces: Creating Room for Personal Healing

Chapter 6: The Hidden Weight: Managing Grief in Professional Spaces

Chapter 7: Compassionate Support: Guiding Others Through Loss

Chapter 8: Honouring Loss: Meaningful Ways to Remember and Connect

Chapter 9: Building Resilience: Gentle Steps Toward Healing

Chapter 10: The Ongoing Journey: Living Meaningfully with Loss

Conclusion

INTRODUCTION

I don't claim to be an expert, but over the years, I have experienced my own losses and supported many others through theirs. Through personal experiences, observations, and professional support training, I have recognized certain behaviours and emotions that often emerge in grief. Writing about these experiences may resonate with you and, hopefully, reassure you that you are not alone.

It's also important to remember that grief isn't only tied to death, loss comes in many forms, each carrying its own weight and impact.

In a world that often urges us to 'move on' from loss, this book offers a different path, one that honours the deeply personal nature of grief. As someone who has walked through the shadows of profound loss and emerged with hard earned wisdom. Each person's journey through grief is unique and shaped by their relationships, experiences, and circumstances.

Grief wears many masks, it may stem from the death of a loved one, the end of a significant relationship, the loss of a career, or even the fading of long held dreams. Each loss carries its own weight, its own challenges, and its own lessons. Yet society often pressures us to process these losses quickly, to return to 'normal' as if grief were a temporary detour rather than a transformative journey.

This book provides a harbour for exploring grief at your

own pace, free from judgment or prescribed timelines. Through these pages, you'll find validation for your experiences and behaviour, practical tools for managing grief's challenges, and gentle guidance for building resilience while honouring your loss. Whether navigating fresh grief or carrying long term loss, these chapters offer insights and strategies that respect your needs and energy levels.

We'll explore how grief manifests in body and mind, affecting everything from sleep patterns to decision making abilities. You'll learn practical techniques for managing grief's cognitive fog, creating healing practices, and maintaining meaningful connections with what you've lost. We'll address the challenges of grieving in a happiness focused culture and provide strategies for setting boundaries that protect your authentic grieving process.

Most importantly, this book acknowledges that grief isn't something to 'get over' but rather an experience to be integrated into your life story. You'll discover ways to honour your loss while gradually building a meaningful life that carries the legacy of what matters most to you. Through real world examples and practical guidance, you'll find support for channelling grief into positive actions that feel authentic to your journey.

As we begin this exploration together, remember that there's no 'right' way to grieve. Your journey is valid, your feelings are legitimate, and your pace is your own. Whether reading this in the depths of fresh loss or seeking guidance for long term grief, these pages offer companionship and practical support for your unique path through loss.

This book isn't about finding quick fixes or easy answers. Instead, it's about developing a deeper understanding of grief's landscape while building a toolkit for navigation that honours both your loss and your continued growth. Together, we'll explore how to carry our grief with meaning, embracing new possibilities for connection, purpose, and hope along the way.

1. THE MANY FACES OF LOSS: UNDERSTANDING DIFFERENT TYPES OF GRIEF

Grief takes on many forms, each as unique and valid as the loss that inspired it. Society often equates grief with death, but loss comes in many forms, each deserving recognition and understanding. Grief speaks many dialects, each shaping our lives in profound ways. Whether it's the void left by the death of a loved one, the aching absence after the end of a significant relationship, the disruption of a career change, or the quiet sorrow of a long held dream slipping away, each loss carries its own weight and deserves its own space in our healing journey.

Grief can also manifest in unexpected ways, as illustrated by a revealing moment in a support group. In a support group, one participant struggled with feeling 'unauthorised' to grieve the loss of their job after a company restructuring. This wasn't just about employment, it marked the end of a 20-year identity, the dissolution of financial security, and the loss of daily connections with colleagues. Initially, they felt guilt for mourning something that wasn't a death. Yet as their story unfolded, others in the group began recognising similar patterns in their own experiences, how the death of a spouse had also meant the loss of future dreams, familiar routines, and social connections. This moment revealed a fundamental truth: grief isn't hierarchical. It is a universal response to change, and every loss deserves space and support.

This experience highlights how different types of loss can intertwine, creating complex layers of grief that require validation and understanding. Whether mourning the tangible loss of a person or the intangible loss of what might have been, every form of grief is real and worthy of care. Recognising this truth is a crucial step in processing our losses and beginning the journey toward healing.

As we explore these many faces of grief, we start to see how loss reshapes our world, sometimes with the stark clarity of a sudden departure, other times creeping in gradually through life transitions. Each symptom of grief carries its own lessons and opportunities for growth, even as we honour the pain it brings.

In the pages ahead, we will examine how different forms of grief present unique challenges and needs. We'll explore how to validate these experiences, whether they align with traditional ideas of loss or challenge our preconceptions about what constitutes "legitimate" grief. Recognising this allows us to develop healthier coping strategies and seek the right support for our journey through loss.

Primary Losses: Understanding Bereavement and Death Related Grief

Grief takes on many forms. For instance, the end of a long-term friendship, the loss of a beloved pet, or even a major life transition like retirement can trigger deep emotional pain. These experiences, though different from bereavement, still carry profound grief that deserves recognition. Society often equates grief with death, but loss comes in many forms, each deserving recognition and understanding. Grief speaks many dialects, each shaping our lives in profound ways. Whether it's the void left by the death of a loved one, the aching absence after the end of a significant relationship, the disruption of a career change, or the quiet sorrow of a long held dream slipping away, each loss carries its own weight and deserves its own space in our healing journey.

When we speak of primary losses, we often refer to the profound grief that accompanies the death of a loved one. This form of loss creates a fundamental rupture in our world, challenging our sense of normalcy and security in ways that can feel overwhelming. The impact reverberates through every aspect of our lives, from our daily routines to our sense of identity and purpose.

Bereavement grief is often displayed in waves that can feel both predictable and surprising. Some days, the weight of loss might feel manageable, while other days, a simple trigger, a familiar scent, a shared memory, or a significant date can bring grief rushing back with unexpected intensity. This ebb and flow is a natural part of the grieving process, not a sign of regression or failure to heal.

The physical and emotional symptoms of bereavement can be intense and varied. Many people experience changes in sleep patterns, appetite fluctuations, difficulty concentrating, and waves of intense emotions that can include sadness, anger, guilt, and even moments of unexpected joy when remembering their loved one. These responses are natural expressions of grief, not signs of weakness or inability to cope.

Common physical symptoms of bereavement:

• Sleep disturbances (insomnia or excessive sleeping)

• Changes in appetite

• Physical fatigue or restlessness

• Heightened sensitivity to noise or light

• Chest tightness or difficulty breathing

Understanding these physical responses can help normalise the experience and reduce anxiety about these natural reactions to loss. Our bodies process grief alongside our hearts and minds, creating a holistic response to profound loss that deserves gentle attention and care.

The social impact of death related grief often creates additional challenges as we navigate changed relationships and roles. The loss of a spouse might mean learning to parent alone, while the loss of a parent might shift family dynamics and responsibilities. These changes require adjustment and patience as we learn to navigate our transformed world.

Key aspects of navigating bereavement:

• Acknowledging the reality of the loss at your own pace

• Finding safe spaces to express grief emotions

• Maintaining basic self-care routines

• Accepting help from support systems

• Creating meaningful ways to honour your loved one

It's crucial to understand that there is no standardised timeline for processing death related grief. While some may feel pressure to 'move on' after a certain period, the reality is that grief often becomes something we learn to carry rather than something we overcome. This understanding can help create space for a more authentic grieving process.

The workplace presents particular challenges when dealing with primary losses. Many organisations offer bereavement leave, but the reality of grief extends far beyond these designated days. Open communication with supervisors about ongoing needs, potential triggers, and temporary accommodations can help create a more supportive environment for processing loss while maintaining professional responsibilities.

One of the most challenging aspects of death related grief is learning to navigate special occasions and milestones. Holidays, anniversaries, and celebrations can trigger intense emotions, making it difficult to participate in events that once brought joy. Planning ahead can help, whether that means setting boundaries around participation, creating new traditions that honour the loved one, or finding quiet moments for personal reflection. Seeking support from trusted friends or family members can also make these occasions more manageable, allowing space for both grief and connection. Holidays, anniversaries, and celebrations can trigger intense grief responses, even years after a loss. Planning for these occasions and creating new traditions that honour both the loss and continuing life can help make these times more manageable.

Remember that seeking professional support for bereavement is not a sign of weakness but often a helpful step in processing profound loss. Grief counsellors and support groups can provide valuable tools and validation for your experience, while also connecting you with others who understand the complexity of death related grief.

As we navigate primary losses, it's essential to remember that each person's grief journey is unique. What brings comfort to one person might not resonate with another, and that's perfectly normal. The key is finding ways to honour your loss and process your grief that feel authentic to you and your relationship with the person who died. What brings comfort to one person might not resonate with another, and that's perfectly normal. The key is finding ways to honour your loss and process your grief that feels authentic to you and your relationship with the person who died.

Secondary Losses: Grief in Life Transitions and Relationship Changes

While primary losses often command our immediate attention, secondary losses the ripple effects that follow major life transitions and relationship changes can create their own profound grief responses that deserve recognition and care. These losses might include divorce, retirement, relocation, health changes, or the end of significant friendships experiences that fundamentally alter our daily lives and sense of identity.

These transitions often trigger a cascade of additional losses that may go unrecognised. For instance, the end of a marriage involves not just the loss of a partner, but potentially the loss of extended family relationships, shared friendships, financial security, and familiar routines. Similarly, retirement might mean losing not only a professional role but also a sense of purpose, daily structure, and workplace relationships that have defined life for decades.

Common secondary losses include:
- Changes in social circles and support systems
- Loss of familiar routines and daily structures
- Shifts in financial circumstances
- Changes in living situations
- Loss of future plans and shared dreams

The grief associated with these secondary losses can be particularly challenging because it often goes unvalidated by others who might view these changes as 'just part of life' or even positive transitions. However, the emotional impact can be just as significant as more traditionally recognised forms of loss.

Life transitions, even when chosen, can trigger genuine grief responses. A promotion at work might bring excitement alongside grief for the team and role being left behind. Moving to a new city for better opportunities might still involve mourning the loss of community and familiar surroundings. Understanding that these feelings of loss are valid, even in the context of positive change, can help us process them more effectively.

Signs of grief in life transitions:
- Feeling disconnected from your new reality
- Unexpected emotional reactions to changes
- Difficulty adapting to new routines
- Longing for previous situations or relationships
- Questioning decisions despite logical benefits

Relationship changes, whether through conscious choice or circumstance, often create complex grief experiences. The end of a friendship, for example, might bring relief from a toxic situation while simultaneously triggering grief for the connection that once existed. These apparently contradictory emotions are normal and deserve space in our healing process.

Navigating secondary losses requires developing new coping strategies and support systems. This might involve creating new routines, finding alternative sources of support, or discovering new ways to meet needs that were previously fulfilled through the lost relationship or situation.

Strategies for managing secondary losses:
- Acknowledging the legitimacy of your grief
- Identifying specific aspects of loss for focused attention
- Creating new rituals and routines
- Building fresh support networks
- Seeking professional guidance when needed

The workplace often becomes a significant arena for managing secondary losses, particularly during career transitions or organisational changes. These situations might require additional support and understanding from management teams who can help create space for processing these transitions while maintaining professional responsibilities.

It's essential to recognise that secondary losses often compound over time, creating layers of grief that need attention and care. Each loss, whether seemingly small or significant, contributes to our overall grief experience and deserves acknowledgment in our healing journey.

As with primary losses, there's no timeline for processing secondary losses. Some changes might be integrated relatively quickly, while others may require longer periods of adjustment and grief work. The key is recognising these experiences as valid forms of loss worthy of our attention and care.

By understanding and validating these secondary losses, we can better support ourselves and others through life's transitions and relationship changes. This recognition helps create space for authentic grieving while developing healthy ways to adapt to our changed circumstances.

Intangible Losses: Grieving Dreams, Identity, and Security
Perhaps the most challenging forms of grief to navigate are those tied to losses we cannot touch, the evaporation of long held dreams, shifts in our sense of self, and the dissolution of security we once took for granted. These intangible losses often go unrecognised by others yet can profoundly impact on our emotional wellbeing and sense of place in the world.

When life events force us to rewrite the stories we've crafted about our future, grief can be particularly complex. A health diagnosis might mean letting go of career aspirations or lifestyle dreams. Financial setbacks could require abandoning plans for education or homeownership. The end of a relationship might mean releasing shared visions of family life or retirement. These invisible losses deserve recognition and space in our grieving process.

Common intangible losses include:
- Future plans and expectations
- Sense of safety and predictability
- Professional identity
- Financial security

- Role within family or community
- Belief systems and worldview

The loss of identity, who we understood ourselves to be often accompanies major life transitions. Whether through retirement, disability, relationship changes, or other circumstances, finding ourselves disconnected from familiar roles can trigger genuine grief responses. This might exhibit as feeling lost, questioning our value, or struggling to envision our place in a changed world.

Security losses, whether financial, emotional, or physical, can fundamentally shake our sense of stability. The grief that accompanies these losses often includes anxiety about the future and mourning for the comfort of certainty we once knew. Even when new forms of security are established, the memory of that lost sense of safety may linger.

Signs of grieving intangible losses:
- Difficulty making future plans
- Feeling disconnected from former roles
- Increased anxiety about the future
- Loss of confidence or self-trust
- Questioning life's meaning or purpose

Processing these invisible losses requires acknowledging their legitimacy and impact. While others might struggle to understand grief for something that never physically existed, these losses can profoundly affect our emotional landscape and deserve careful attention in our healing journey.

Navigating intangible losses often requires developing new frameworks for understanding ourselves and our place in the world. This might involve exploring new sources of meaning, building fresh support systems, or discovering alternative ways to fulfil our needs for purpose and belonging.

Strategies for managing intangible losses:

- Journaling about identity changes
- Creating new rituals for security
- Connecting with others experiencing similar transitions
- Exploring new sources of meaning
- Building flexible plans for the future

The workplace often becomes a crucial arena for processing intangible losses, particularly when they involve professional identity or security changes. Open communication with management about these challenges can help create understanding and support while maintaining professional responsibilities.

It's essential to recognise that intangible losses often layer upon each other, creating complex grief experiences that need time and attention to process. Each loss, whether visible to others or not, contributes to our overall grief experience and deserves acknowledgment in our healing journey.

As we navigate these invisible losses, remember that their intangible nature doesn't make them any less real or significant. By acknowledging and honouring these losses, we can begin to build new dreams, discover evolved identities, and create different forms of security that align with our changed circumstances. As we conclude our exploration of grief's many faces, it becomes clear that loss touches our lives in ways both expected and surprising. Through the stories shared in support groups and individual experiences, we've seen how grief defies simple categorisation, appearing not just in the wake of death but in the midst of life's various transitions and changes.

The journey through this chapter has revealed several essential truths about grief and loss. First, that all forms of grief whether from bereavement, life transitions, or intangible losses deserve validation and care. Second, that grief often creates ripple effects, touching multiple aspects of our lives simultaneously. And third, understanding these different symptoms of grief can help us better support ourselves and others through times of loss.

Perhaps most importantly, we've learned that grief isn't a hierarchy where some losses matter more than others. Whether mourning the death of a loved one, adjusting to a career transition, or processing the loss of a long-held dream, each experience of grief carries its own weight and deserves acknowledgment. This understanding opens the door to more compassionate and inclusive support for all who navigate the complex terrain of loss.

As we move forward, remember that recognising these various forms of grief is just the first step. Each type of loss may require different coping strategies and support systems, but all benefit from patient understanding and gentle acceptance. By acknowledging the legitimacy of our grief, whatever its source, we create space for authentic healing and growth.

In the chapters ahead, we'll explore specific tools and strategies for navigating these different types of grief, always remembering that each person's journey through loss is unique and valid. Whether you're experiencing primary losses, secondary transitions, or intangible changes, your grief matters and deserves care and attention.

Remember that understanding grief's many faces doesn't make the journey easier, but it can help us feel less alone and more prepared to navigate its challenges. As we continue through this book, we'll build on this foundation, exploring practical ways to honour our losses while gradually building meaningful lives that carry both our grief and our hope for the future.

2. RECOGNISING GRIEF BEHAVIOURS: YOUR BODY'S RESPONSE TO LOSS

Our bodies hold the weight of grief in ways that often surprise and sometimes alarm us, speaking a language of loss that appears in physical sensations and behavioural changes. Like waves that reshape a shoreline, grief gradually alters our daily patterns from how we sleep to how we eat, from our energy levels to our ability to focus. Whether it's the sudden racing of our heart when a memory surfaces unexpectedly, or the profound exhaustion that makes even simple tasks feel overwhelming, our bodies create a physical narrative of our grief that deserves both recognition and gentle care.

This physical response to loss displays differently for each person, yet common patterns emerge in how our bodies process grief. From disrupted sleep patterns to changes in appetite, from moments of intense energy to periods of complete exhaustion, our bodies speak the language of loss in ways that often catch us off guard. These reactions aren't signs of weakness or failure; they're natural responses to the profound impact of loss on our entire being.

In grief support settings, it's common to hear people express confusion and concern about their physical symptoms after loss. A support group participant shared their experience of completely losing their appetite, struggling with insomnia, and feeling physically exhausted despite minimal activity. As they described these symptoms, other group members began nodding in recognition. What followed was a profound discussion about how grief manifests in the body, one person described feeling like they were moving through thick fog, another talked about forgetting simple tasks they'd done hundreds of times before. Through their shared experiences, the group members realised that what they had individually attributed to 'something wrong with them' was actually their body's natural response to grief. This revelation brought immense relief and opened the door to discussing practical coping strategies for managing these physical symptoms of grief.

Understanding these physical responses can help us approach our grieving bodies with greater compassion and awareness. Just as grief itself doesn't follow a linear path, our body's response to loss may fluctuate, some days feeling more manageable than others. This chapter explores these physical symptoms of grief, offering insights into why they occur and practical strategies for managing them with gentleness and understanding.

By recognising and honouring these physical aspects of grief, we can begin to develop a more comprehensive approach to our healing journey. Rather than fighting against our body's natural responses to loss, we can learn to work with them, creating space for both the physical and emotional aspects of our grief process. This understanding forms the foundation for developing effective coping strategies that respect both our body's needs and our unique grieving style.

Physical Symptoms: Understanding Common Bodily Responses to Grief

When grief enters our lives, it often announces itself through profound physical symptoms that can be both surprising and concerning. Our bodies respond to emotional pain in tangible ways, creating a complex web of physical symptoms that deserve our attention and understanding.

Common physical responses to grief include:
- Sleep disturbances (insomnia or excessive sleeping)
- Changes in appetite and digestion
- Muscle tension and physical aches
- Fatigue and decreased energy
- Weakened immune system
- Heart palpitations or chest tightness

These physical symptoms aren't just side effects of grief, they're integral parts of how our bodies process loss. When we understand these responses as natural rather than problematic, we can approach them with greater patience and self-compassion.

The connection between emotional pain and physical symptoms often manifests in our daily routines. Many people experience heaviness in their chest or a knot in their stomach when grief waves hit. Others notice their hands trembling when handling objects that trigger memories or find themselves taking shallow breaths when passing places associated with their loss. These reactions stem from our body's stress response system, which activates during emotional distress just as it does during physical danger.

Sleep often becomes a particular challenge during grief, with many people experiencing dramatic changes in their sleep patterns. Some find themselves unable to fall asleep, lying awake with racing thoughts and memories. Others may sleep excessively, using sleep as an escape from overwhelming emotions. Both responses are normal ways our bodies attempt to cope with loss.

Another significant physical symptom appears in our eating patterns. Some people lose their appetite entirely, finding food tasteless or feeling too nauseous to eat. Others may experience increased appetite, turning to food for comfort or distraction. These changes in eating habits can then affect our energy levels, creating a cycle that impacts on our overall physical wellbeing.

Practical strategies for managing physical symptoms include:
- Maintaining regular mealtimes, even if portions are smaller
- Creating a consistent sleep routine with relaxing bedtime rituals
- Gentle physical movement like walking or stretching
- Regular hydration and basic nutrition
- Brief rest periods throughout the day

It's important to note that while these physical symptoms are normal, persistent or severe symptoms should be discussed with healthcare providers. Grief can impact our physical health significantly, and there's no shame in seeking medical support when needed. Healthcare providers can help distinguish between normal grief responses and symptoms that might need additional attention.

The workplace often becomes a challenging environment when dealing with these physical symptoms. Simple tasks may suddenly require more energy, and concentration might prove difficult. For managers and colleagues, understanding these physical impacts of grief can help create more supportive work environments. This might include allowing flexible break times, providing quiet spaces for rest, or adjusting workloads temporarily.

Remember that these physical responses to grief typically ebb and flow, just like emotional responses. Some days may bring more pronounced symptoms than others. This fluctuation is normal and doesn't indicate a setback in the grieving process. Instead, it reflects the natural rhythm of how our bodies process and adapt to loss over time.

Cognitive Changes: Managing Memory, Focus, and Decision Making During Loss

One of the most challenging aspects of grief is its impact on our cognitive functions, the way we think, remember, and make decisions. Often described as 'grief brain' or 'grief fog,' these cognitive changes can make even familiar tasks feel overwhelming and complex decisions seem impossible to navigate.

Common cognitive changes during grief include:
- Difficulty concentrating or maintaining focus
- Memory lapses and forgetfulness
- Challenges with decision making
- Confusion with routine tasks
- Slower processing of information
- Difficulty organising thoughts or plans

These cognitive changes aren't signs of weakness or permanent impairment; they're natural responses to the overwhelming nature of loss. When our minds are processing grief, they often have less capacity for other cognitive tasks, like how a computer might run slower when processing a large file.

Understanding these cognitive changes can help us approach them with greater patience and develop practical strategies for managing daily life. Many people report feeling frustrated when they can't remember important dates, lose track of conversations, or struggle to make simple decisions. This frustration often compounds when others don't understand why previously simple tasks now feel overwhelming.

Practical strategies for managing cognitive changes include:
- Breaking tasks into smaller, manageable steps
- Using written reminders and lists

- Scheduling important tasks during peak energy times
- Limiting major decisions when possible
- Creating simple routines for daily tasks
- Setting alarms for important reminders

In professional settings, these cognitive changes can be particularly challenging. Tasks that once felt routine might suddenly require intense concentration, and complex projects may feel overwhelming. It's important for both grieving individuals and their managers to understand these changes and implement appropriate support strategies.

For managers supporting grieving team members, consider:
- Providing written instructions for tasks
- Breaking projects into smaller components
- Scheduling regular check ins
- Creating backup systems for important deadlines
- Allowing flexible work arrangements when possible
- Reducing cognitive load during peak grief periods

Decision making often becomes particularly challenging during grief. The combination of emotional overwhelm and cognitive fog can make even simple choices feel impossible.

When facing important decisions, consider implementing a structured approach:
- Delay major decisions when possible
- Break decisions into smaller components
- Seek trusted input when needed
- Write down pros and cons
- Give yourself permission to change your mind

Memory challenges during grief can be especially distressing when they involve memories of the person or thing we've lost. Some people worry that forgetting small details means they're losing their connection to their loved one. However, these memory fluctuations are normal and often temporary. Creating memory books, journals, or digital archives can help preserve important memories while reducing the pressure to keep everything in mind.

The cognitive impacts of grief often follow a wave like pattern, with some days feeling clearer than others. This inconsistency is normal and doesn't indicate a lack of progress. Instead, it reflects how our brains naturally process loss while trying to maintain daily functioning. Understanding this pattern can help reduce self-judgment and allow for more flexible approaches to managing cognitive challenges.

As with physical symptoms, persistent or severe cognitive changes should be discussed with healthcare providers. While cognitive changes are normal during grief, having professional support can help distinguish between typical grief responses and situations that might need additional attention. Healthcare providers can offer strategies for managing these changes and ensure other factors aren't contributing to cognitive difficulties.

Remember that these cognitive changes typically improve gradually as we learn to integrate our loss. In the meantime, approaching ourselves with patience and understanding can help us navigate this challenging aspect of grief. Creating systems and routines that support our changed cognitive capacity isn't admitting defeat, it's a practical way to care for ourselves while our minds process loss.

Sleep and Energy: Navigating Rest and Activity While Grieving
Sleep and energy levels often become significant challenges during grief, creating a complex cycle that can impact our overall wellbeing. The relationship between grief and rest isn't straightforward as grief can be exhausting, it frequently disrupts our natural sleep patterns and energy rhythms.

Common sleep related challenges during grief include:
- Difficulty falling asleep
- Frequent waking during the night
- Vivid dreams or nightmares
- Oversleeping as an escape

- Restless, unrefreshing sleep
- Daytime fatigue despite adequate sleep hours

These sleep disruptions stem from both emotional and physical aspects of grief. Our minds may become more active at night, replaying memories or processing emotions when external distractions fade. Meanwhile, stress hormones released during grief can interfere with our natural sleep wake cycle, making it harder to maintain consistent rest patterns.

Energy levels during grief often follow an unpredictable pattern. Some days might bring intense bursts of nervous energy, while others leave us struggling to accomplish basic tasks. This fluctuation is normal and reflects our body's ongoing process of adapting to loss. Understanding these energy patterns can help us plan our activities more effectively and avoid overextending ourselves during vulnerable periods.

Practical strategies for managing sleep and energy include:
- Maintaining consistent sleep and wake times
- Creating a calming bedtime routine
- Limiting screen time before bed
- Using relaxation techniques like deep breathing
- Planning important tasks during peak energy times
- Taking short rest breaks throughout the day

In professional settings, managing energy levels requires careful attention. Supervisors can support grieving team members by:
- Allowing flexible scheduling when possible
- Providing quiet spaces for brief rest periods
- Adjusting workload during low energy periods
- Understanding that productivity may fluctuate
- Supporting breaks when needed

Physical activity plays a crucial role in managing both sleep and energy levels during grief. While exercise might feel overwhelming initially, gentle movement can help regulate sleep patterns and boost natural energy. Simple activities like short walks, gentle stretching, or basic yoga poses can provide benefits without overwhelming depleted energy reserves.

It's important to recognise that grief requires significant energy both emotional and physical. This means we often need more rest than usual, even if we're not engaging in our typical activities. Giving ourselves permission to rest without guilt is an essential part of the grieving process.

When sleep problems persist, consider:
- Consulting healthcare providers about temporary sleep support
- Creating a sleep friendly environment (cool, dark, quiet)
- Establishing regular mealtimes to support natural rhythms
- Limiting caffeine and alcohol, especially later in the day
- Journaling before bed to release troubling thoughts

Energy management during grief involves learning to pace ourselves differently. Rather than pushing through fatigue, we need to respect our body's changing needs and adjust our expectations accordingly. This might mean breaking tasks into smaller segments, scheduling rest periods, or saying no to non-essential commitments.

Some days we will naturally have more energy than others. Creating a flexible routine that can adapt to these fluctuations helps prevent exhaustion while maintaining some sense of structure. This might include identifying essential tasks that need consistent attention while allowing other activities to shift based on energy levels.

Remember that sleep and energy patterns typically stabilise gradually as we adjust to our loss. In the meantime, approaching these challenges with patience and self-compassion helps us maintain basic functioning while honouring our body's need for rest during this demanding time. As we conclude this exploration of grief's physical and cognitive symptoms, it becomes clear that our bodies speak profound language of loss that deserves both recognition and gentle care. The physical symptoms and behavioural changes we experience aren't signs of weakness or failure, but rather natural responses to the deep impact of loss on our entire being.

Through understanding how grief affects our bodies, minds, and energy levels, we can begin to develop more compassionate and effective ways of caring for ourselves during this challenging time. The fog of grief that impacts our memory, the exhaustion that weaves through our days, and the disrupted sleep patterns that often accompany loss are all part of our body's process of adapting to significant change.

Key takeaways from this chapter include understanding that grief appears physically in various ways:

- Physical symptoms like fatigue, appetite changes, and sleep disruptions are normal responses to loss
- Cognitive changes, including difficulty concentrating and memory challenges, are common and temporary
- Energy levels naturally fluctuate during grief, requiring flexible approaches to daily tasks
- Sleep patterns may shift dramatically, needing patient and consistent attention
- Workplace accommodations might be necessary to support these physical and cognitive changes

Remember that these physical and cognitive responses typically ebb and flow, just like emotional aspects of grief. Some days will feel more manageable than others, and that's okay. The key is not to fight against these natural responses but to collaborate with them, developing strategies that honour both our grief and our need to function in daily life.

As we move forward, consider how this understanding of grief's physical impact can help shape more compassionate approaches to self-care and support systems. Recognising these bodily responses as valid and normal can help reduce the additional stress of wondering 'what's wrong with me?' and instead focus energy on gentle, practical coping strategies.

In the chapters ahead, we'll explore more specific tools for navigating these physical and emotional aspects of grief, always remembering that each person's experience is unique and deserving of respect. The body's grief language, while sometimes challenging, ultimately serves as a guide in our healing journey, helping us understand when to push forward and when to rest.

For now, take comfort in knowing that your body's responses to grief, however they manifest, are part of your unique processing of loss. As you continue reading, keep building your understanding of these responses and gathering tools to support yourself through this significant transition.

3. NAVIGATING THE FOG: ESSENTIAL TOOLS FOR MINDFUL MOURNING

When grief descends like a heavy fog, even the simplest tasks can feel overwhelming and disorienting. Yet within this fog lies opportunities to develop gentle awareness and self-compassion that can help us navigate through our most challenging moments. The journey through grief often feels like walking through a dense fog where familiar landmarks become obscured, and each step forward requires careful consideration. Yet within this fog lies an opportunity to develop a deeper connection with ourselves and our grieving process through mindful awareness.

Mindfulness in grief isn't about forcing happiness or suppressing pain, it's about creating space to experience our emotions fully while maintaining a gentle awareness that helps us stay grounded in the present moment. This balanced approach allows us to navigate the intensity of grief while preventing ourselves from becoming completely overwhelmed by it.

This delicate balance was beautifully illustrated in a grief support workshop where participants discovered the power of simple grounding techniques using everyday objects. One participant's experience with a smooth river stone became a powerful testament to how mindful awareness can transform ordinary moments into meaningful anchors during grief. By focusing on the stone's texture and temperature when grief waves hit during work meetings, they found a way to stay present without denying their emotions.

What began as a simple grounding technique evolved into a profound daily ritual a few minutes each morning holding the stone while acknowledging both their grief and their capacity to carry it through another day. This practice demonstrated how mindful awareness could provide a bridge between the need to function in daily life and the ongoing process of grieving, especially in settings where obvious expressions of mourning might feel uncomfortable.

In this chapter, we'll explore practical mindfulness techniques specifically designed for those experiencing grief. These tools aren't meant to diminish or rush through your grief but rather to help you stay present with it in ways that feel manageable and meaningful. We'll look at simple grounding exercises that can help during overwhelming moments, breathing techniques that can serve as anchors during grief storms, and ways to create daily rituals that honour both your loss and your need to move through each day.

Remember that mindfulness in grief isn't about achieving a particular state of mind or following strict rules. Instead, it's about finding gentle ways to stay present with your experience while creating space for both your pain and your healing. Some days, this might mean simply acknowledging your grief without trying to change it. Other days, it might involve actively using grounding techniques to help you navigate challenging situations.

As we explore these tools and practices, keep in mind that you can adapt them to fit your needs and energy levels. The goal isn't perfection but rather finding what works for you in different moments of your grief journey. Through mindful awareness, we can learn to navigate the fog of grief with more ease, not by pushing it away, but by developing skills to move through it with greater understanding and self-compassion.

Grounding Techniques: Simple Tools for Managing Overwhelming Moments

When grief overwhelms us, our bodies and minds can feel disconnected from the present moment, making even simple tasks feel insurmountable. Grounding techniques offer practical tools to help anchor ourselves during these challenging times, bringing gentle awareness back to the present moment without denying or suppressing our grief.

Here are several simple yet effective grounding techniques that can help manage overwhelming moments:

- The 5 4 3 2 1 Sensory Exercise: Name five things you can see, four things you can touch, three things you can hear, two things you can smell, and one thing you can taste
- Deep breathing with hand on heart: Place one hand on your heart, the other on your belly, and take slow, gentle breaths
- Object anchoring: Hold a meaningful object, focusing on its texture, temperature, and weight
- Gentle movement: Simple stretches or walking mindfully, noticing each step
- Cold water contact: Running cool water over your hands or holding a cold object

These techniques work by engaging our senses and bringing attention to the present moment, helping to calm our nervous system when grief feels overwhelming. They're particularly valuable in public settings or professional environments where we need to regain composure quickly.

One support group participant found that keeping a small box of grounding tools at their desk helped them navigate difficult moments at work. The box contained items with different sensory qualities a smooth stone, a scented handkerchief, a small photo, and a piece of textured fabric. Having these tools readily available provided comfort and stability during unexpected waves of grief.

It's important to remember that grounding techniques aren't meant to eliminate or suppress grief emotions rather, they help us stay present with our experience in a way that feels manageable. Think of them as temporary anchors during emotional storms, providing just enough stability to weather intense moments.

Practicing these techniques when you're feeling relatively calm can help make them more effective during challenging times. Start with short periods, even 30 seconds of mindful breathing or sensory awareness can be effective. As you become more familiar with these tools, you can adapt and modify them to better suit your needs.

- Create environmental anchors: Set up specific spots at home or work with grounding objects
- Use time limited approaches: Set a gentle timer for grounding exercises to prevent overwhelm
- Combine techniques: Mix physical and mental grounding tools based on what feels most helpful

Remember that different techniques may work better on different days or in different situations. What helps during a quiet moment at home might not be practical during a work meeting. Having several options allows you to respond flexibly to your needs as they change.

The effectiveness of grounding techniques often lies in their simplicity. When grief clouds our thinking, complex strategies can feel overwhelming. These straightforward tools provide accessible ways to regain our footing without requiring extensive energy or concentration.

Many people find it helpful to write down their preferred grounding techniques and keep the list easily accessible, perhaps on their phone or in a small notebook. This removes the need to remember specific steps during overwhelming moments when recall might be difficult.

While these techniques can provide immediate relief during intense moments, they work best as part of a larger self-care strategy. Combined with other mindful practices, support systems, and professional help when needed, grounding techniques become valuable tools in our grief journey, helping us navigate difficult moments while honouring our ongoing process of healing.

Mindful Breathing: Anchoring Yourself During Grief Storms
Our breath remains a constant companion through life's storms, including the turbulent waves of grief. When loss leaves us feeling unmoored, conscious breathing can serve as a gentle anchor, helping us stay present even when emotions feel overwhelming.

Breathing mindfully during grief isn't about controlling or changing our experience it's about creating a stable foundation from which to feel our emotions safely. This practice becomes particularly valuable when grief storms arise unexpectedly in public settings or during times when we need to maintain some level of functioning.

Here are several simple breathing techniques that can help during intense moments of grief:
- Square Breathing: Inhale for four counts, hold for four, exhale for four, hold for four
- Ocean Breath: Make a gentle sound like waves while breathing deeply
- Hand Heart Connection: Place one hand on your heart while breathing slowly
- Counting Breaths: Count each exhale up to ten, then start again
- Bubble Breathing: Imagine your breath as gentle bubbles rising and falling

These techniques work best when practiced regularly during calmer moments, building familiarity that makes them more accessible during difficult times. Start with just a few minutes at a time grief can make it challenging to focus for longer periods.

In a grief support workshop, participants discovered how conscious breathing could create small pockets of peace within their day. One participant found that taking three mindful breaths before entering their workplace helped them transition between their private grieving space and professional environment. Another developed a practice of breathing with their hand on their heart while looking at their loved one's photo, creating a daily ritual of connection and grounding.

It's important to remember that mindful breathing isn't about suppressing grief emotions or trying to 'calm down.' Instead, it offers a way to be present with our feelings while maintaining enough stability to prevent becoming completely overwhelmed. Think of it as creating a sturdy container that can hold both your grief and your need to function in daily life.

When using breathing techniques during grief, consider these supportive practices:
- Find a comfortable position that feels sustainable
- Keep your eyes open or closed based on what feels safer
- Start with short periods and gradually extend as comfortable
- Use gentle counting or visualisation if it helps maintain focus
- Release any expectations about 'doing it right'

Mindful breathing can be particularly helpful during grief triggers or anniversary dates. Having this tool available doesn't mean you won't feel intense emotions, but it can help you move through them with more stability and self-compassion.

Some people find it helpful to pair their breathing practice with simple phrases or intentions. During the inhale, you might silently say 'I am here,' and during the exhale, 'I can hold this.' These phrases acknowledge both your presence in the current moment and your capacity to carry grief.

Remember that like all aspects of grief, your relationship with breathing practices may change over time. What feels supportive one day might not work the next. Allow yourself to adapt these techniques to your needs, treating them as flexible tools rather than rigid rules.

Through consistent, gentle practice, mindful breathing can become a reliable companion in your grief journey not as a way to escape your feelings, but as a means of staying present with them while maintaining your foundation. This balance helps create space for both honouring your loss and caring for yourself as you navigate each day.

Creating Mindful Rituals: Daily Practices for Processing Loss
Creating mindful rituals provides structure and meaning during times when grief makes each day feel overwhelming. These intentional practices offer gentle ways to acknowledge our loss while gradually building new patterns that support our healing journey.

In grief support settings, participants often express feeling lost without their familiar routines or struggling to find meaningful ways to structure their days. Creating simple, sustainable rituals can help anchor us during these challenging times, providing touchstones throughout our day that honour both our grief and our need to move forward.

Here are several mindful rituals that can be incorporated into daily life:
- Morning acknowledgment: Begin each day with a quiet moment of reflection, perhaps lighting a candle or looking at a photo
- Gratitude pairing: Combine grief acknowledgment with noting one small thing you appreciate
- Evening reflection: End your day by writing briefly about your feelings or memories
- Nature connection: Spend a few minutes outdoors, observing seasonal changes
- Memory moments: Set aside specific times to look at photos or remember stories

The key to establishing helpful grief rituals lies in their simplicity and sustainability. Rather than creating elaborate ceremonies that require significant energy, focus on small, manageable practices that can be maintained even on difficult days.

A grief support group participant shared how they transformed their morning coffee routine into a mindful ritual. Instead of rushing through breakfast, they began sitting quietly with their coffee, using this time to acknowledge their feelings and prepare for the day ahead. This simple change provided a gentle way to create space for grief while maintaining daily function.

When developing personal rituals, consider these guiding principles:
- Start small: Begin with one simple practice rather than multiple complex ones
- Be flexible: Allow rituals to evolve as your needs change
- Stay consistent: Choose times or triggers that naturally fit your schedule
- Honour your energy: Create practices that match your current capacity
- Include sensory elements: Incorporate meaningful objects, scents, or sounds

Remember that rituals don't need to be sombre or serious, they can include elements of joy, creativity, or playfulness while still honouring your loss. Some find comfort in gardening rituals, others in artistic practices or music. The key is finding what resonates with your personal grieving style.

Creating mindful rituals also helps us navigate the challenge of maintaining connections with our lost loved ones while building new patterns of living. These practices can serve as bridges between our past and present, allowing us to carry memories forward in meaningful ways.

One particularly helpful approach involves creating transition rituals, small practices that help us move between different aspects of our day. These might include taking three mindful breaths before entering the workplace, touching a meaningful object before important meetings, or having a quiet moment of remembrance before social events.

When establishing grief rituals, be mindful of these common pitfalls:
- Avoid making practices too complex or time consuming
- Don't create rituals that isolate you from needed support
- Be careful not to let rituals become rigid rules that increase anxiety
- Remember that it's okay to modify or release rituals that no longer serve you

The power of mindful rituals lies not in their perfection but in their ability to provide gentle structure during a time when life feels chaotic. They offer ways to acknowledge our grief while gradually building new patterns that support our healing journey.

Through consistent, simple practices, we can create touchstones throughout our day that honour both our loss and our continued living. These rituals become companions in our grief journey, helping us navigate each day with more intention and self-compassion while maintaining meaningful connections to what we've lost. As we conclude this chapter on mindful mourning, it's important to remember that navigating the fog of grief doesn't require complex solutions or perfect practices. The simple tools and techniques we've explored, from grounding exercises to mindful breathing and daily rituals offer practical ways to stay present with our grief while maintaining our ability to function in daily life.

Through the experiences shared in grief support settings, we've seen how even small practices can make a significant difference. The participant who found solace in holding a river stone during difficult meetings demonstrated how simple objects can become powerful anchors. Their experience shows us that mindful awareness doesn't require elaborate techniques, sometimes the most effective tools are the ones we can easily access and integrate into our daily routines.

The fog of grief may persist, coming and going like waves on a beach, but these mindful practices provide reliable touchstones we can return to again and again. They help us create moments of stability without denying or suppressing our grief emotions. Whether it's taking three conscious breaths before entering a challenging situation, holding a meaningful object during difficult moments, or creating simple daily rituals that honour our loss, these practices offer gentle ways to stay grounded while processing our grief.

Remember that mindfulness in grief isn't about achieving a particular state or following strict rules. Instead, it's about finding accessible ways to acknowledge and be present with our experience while maintaining enough stability to move through each day. Some days, this might mean simply noting our grief without trying to change it. Other days, it might involve actively using grounding techniques to help us navigate challenging situations.

As you continue your grief journey, consider which practices resonate most strongly with you. Perhaps it's the sensory awareness exercises that help during overwhelming moments, or maybe the creation of small daily rituals provides the structure you need. Whatever tools you choose, remember that they're meant to support rather than suppress your grieving process.

The fog of grief is real, and its density can make even simple tasks feel overwhelming. But through mindful awareness and gentle practices, we can develop the capacity to navigate this fog while honouring our loss. These tools don't eliminate our grief nor should they, but they can help us carry it more sustainably as we continue our journey of healing.

May these practices serve as faithful companions as you navigate your unique path through grief, offering moments of clarity and stability when the fog feels thickest. Remember that each small step in mindful awareness contributes to your overall journey of healing, even on days when progress feels impossible to measure.

4. BREAKING THE TIMELINE: PERMISSION TO GRIEVE AT YOUR OWN PACE

Society often presents grief as a linear journey with clear stages and expected timelines, but the reality of loss defies such neat categorisation. Your grief journey is as unique as your fingerprint, shaped by your relationship with what was lost, your personal history, and the circumstances surrounding your loss. The expectations we face about how and when we should grieve often come from well-meaning sources, family members who want to see us 'happy again,' colleagues who need our full attention back at work, or a culture that celebrates quick emotional recovery as strength. Yet these external pressures can create additional burdens during an already challenging journey.

Consider how grief displays differently for each person, influenced by factors such as cultural background, personal history, and the nature of the loss itself. Some may find solace in returning to routine quickly, while others need extended time to process their emotions. Both approaches are equally valid and deserve respect.

This truth becomes particularly evident in workplace settings, where the intersection of professional expectations and personal grief can create unique challenges. During a workplace grief support session, a team member's experience highlighted this complex dynamic. Their struggle with returning to work after losing their spouse revealed how societal expectations often clash with the reality of grief's timeline. While some colleagues expected an immediate return to 'normal' after bereavement leave, others awkwardly avoided any mention of loss or family, creating an additional emotional burden.

Through collaboration with their manager, they developed a flexible approach that honoured both their professional responsibilities and their need to grieve. This included options for working from home when grief waves hit strongly and designated times for grief processing, such as taking private lunch breaks for journaling or emotional release. Their experience demonstrates how creating space for grief within daily life, rather than trying to 'move past it,' can support both professional functioning and authentic grieving.

This arrangement illustrates a crucial truth about grief, it doesn't conform to external timelines or expectations. Instead, it requires us to find ways to honour our personal grieving needs within practical constraints. The pressure to 'return to normal' often overlooks how profoundly loss can change our perspective and needs.

By understanding that grief doesn't follow a prescribed timeline, we can begin to advocate for our own healing journey. This might mean setting boundaries with well-meaning friends, adjusting work arrangements, or simply giving ourselves permission to experience grief differently from others. What matters most is finding a path that feels authentic to our own experience of loss, even if it doesn't match others' expectations.

In the chapters ahead, we'll explore practical strategies for managing these external pressures while honouring your unique grieving process. You'll learn how to create boundaries that protect your healing journey, communicate your needs effectively, and find support that respects your individual timeline. Remember, there is no universal roadmap for grief your journey is uniquely yours, and you have the right to navigate it at your own pace.

Resisting the Pressure: Managing External Expectations About Grief

One of the most challenging aspects of grief is managing the expectations and pressures that come from those around us. These pressures often manifest in well-intentioned but potentially harmful phrases like 'you need to stay strong,' 'it's time to move on,' or 'they wouldn't want you to be sad.' While these comments typically come from a place of care, they can create additional stress during an already difficult time.

Understanding and managing these external pressures requires developing specific strategies and responses. Here are some common sources of pressure and ways to handle them:
- Family members who expect you to maintain traditional roles or responsibilities
- Friends who want to see you 'back to normal'
- Workplace expectations about productivity and emotional expression
- Cultural or religious expectations about appropriate grieving behaviours
- Social media pressure to present a certain image or timeline of recovery

Learning to resist these pressures starts with recognising that your grief journey belongs to you. This means developing the confidence to set boundaries and communicate your needs clearly. When someone suggests you should be 'moving on,' it's perfectly acceptable to respond with statements like 'I'm taking the time I need' or 'I appreciate your concern, but I need to process this in my own way.'

Creating a support system that understands and respects your grieving process is crucial. This might mean connecting with others who have experienced similar losses, working with a grief counsellor, or joining support groups where your experience is validated. These spaces can provide refuge from societal pressure while offering tools for managing external expectations.

It's important to recognise that resistance to external pressure doesn't mean isolation or rejection of support. Instead, it means being selective about the type of support you accept and setting clear boundaries around how others interact with your grief. This might involve educating those close to you about grief's individual nature or providing them with specific ways they can help that align with your needs.

Sometimes, the pressure we face comes from internalised expectations about how we 'should' be grieving. These internal pressures often reflect societal messages about strength, resilience, and recovery. Challenging these internalised expectations is just as important as managing external ones. Remember that taking time to grieve, expressing emotions openly, and moving at your own pace are signs of self-awareness and self-respect, not weakness.

Workplace environments can be particularly challenging when it comes to grief expectations. Consider developing a clear communication strategy with your supervisor and colleagues. This might include:
- Setting realistic expectations about your capacity and energy levels
- Identifying specific accommodations that would support your grief process
- Establishing boundaries around personal conversations about your loss
- Creating a plan for handling emotional moments during work hours

Remember that protecting your grieving process isn't selfish, it's necessary for genuine healing. When you feel pressured to conform to others' expectations, pause and ask yourself what you truly need in that moment. Your answers might change from day to day, and that's perfectly normal.

Developing a set of prepared responses can help when facing unwanted advice or pressure. These might include phrases like 'Thank you for your concern, but I'm finding my own way through this' or 'I know you want to help, but what I need most right now is space to process this in my own time.' These responses acknowledge others' good intentions while firmly maintaining your boundaries.

The journey through grief is deeply personal, and no one else can determine its proper course or timeline. By resisting external pressure to grieve in prescribed ways, you create space for authentic healing and honour the unique nature of your loss. This resistance isn't about pushing people away but about creating the conditions you need for genuine healing and growth at your own pace.

Understanding Grief Cycles: The Non Linear Nature of Loss
One of the most important truths about grief is that it rarely follows a straight path. Instead of moving steadily from one stage to the next, grief often moves in cycles, with periods of intense emotion followed by times of relative calm. This cyclical nature can be particularly challenging when we expect grief to follow a more linear progression.

Many people experience what we might call 'grief waves', moments when loss feels as fresh and raw as it did in the beginning, months or even years later. These waves can be triggered by:
- Significant dates or anniversaries
- Familiar places or activities
- Songs, scents, or other sensory reminders
- Major life events or milestones
- Unexpected memories or associations

Understanding the cyclical nature of grief can help normalise these experiences and reduce the self-judgment that often accompanies them. When we expect grief to move in only one direction, forward, we may feel we're 'doing it wrong' when intense emotions resurface. However, these recurring waves of grief are not signs of failure or lack of progress; they're natural parts of processing loss.

The intensity and frequency of grief cycles often change over time, though not necessarily in predictable ways. Some people describe their grief as being like a spiral, while they may revisit similar emotions or memories, they do so from slightly different perspectives as time passes. This gradual shift in perspective can allow for new insights and understanding, even as the core experience of loss remains.

It's particularly important to recognise how grief cycles can affect daily functioning. During more intense periods, you might notice:
- Changes in energy levels and concentration
- Shifts in appetite or sleep patterns
- Increased emotional sensitivity
- Temporary difficulty with routine tasks
- Need for more solitude or support

Preparing for these cycles can help make them more manageable. Consider developing a 'grief toolkit', strategies and resources you can draw upon when waves of grief intensify. This might include:
- Flexible self-care practices that adapt to your energy levels
- A list of understanding friends or family members you can reach out to
- Simple grounding techniques for overwhelming moments
- Permission slips for adjusting commitments when needed

The workplace can be particularly challenging when navigating grief cycles. Having open communication with supervisors about the unpredictable nature of grief can help establish needed flexibility. This might include creating contingency plans for days when grief is more intense or identifying specific accommodations that support your healing process.

It's also valuable to recognise that grief cycles often coincide with growth and healing. Just as nature moves through seasons, our grief journey includes periods of both intense emotion and relative calm. These cycles can provide opportunities for processing various aspects of our loss, integrating new understanding, and gradually building resilience.

Rather than fighting against the cyclical nature of grief, we can learn to work with it. This might mean developing strategies for riding the waves when they come, while also recognising that calmer waters will return. Some find it helpful to keep a simple grief journal, noting patterns in their grief cycles and identifying what helps during distinct phases.

Remember that each person's grief cycles will look different, influenced by factors like personality, circumstances of the loss, and available support systems. There's no universal timeline or pattern that grief must follow. Your journey is valid, even if it doesn't match others' experiences or expectations.

By understanding and accepting the non linear nature of grief, we can approach our healing journey with more patience and self-compassion. This understanding helps us resist the pressure to 'get over it' and instead focus on learning to live with our loss in ways that honour both our past connections and our continuing growth.

Creating Boundaries: Protecting Your Right to Grieve
Setting and maintaining healthy boundaries is essential for protecting your grieving process and emotional wellbeing. These boundaries serve as invisible shields that create safe spaces for you to experience and express your grief authentically, without interference from others' expectations or demands.

One of the most crucial aspects of establishing boundaries is learning to recognise when they're needed. Common situations that may require boundary setting include:
- Well-meaning friends who offer unsolicited advice
- Family members who pressure you to 'get back to normal'

- Colleagues who ask invasive questions about your loss
- Social obligations that feel overwhelming
- Requests that exceed your current emotional capacity

Setting boundaries doesn't mean pushing people away or isolating yourself. Instead, it means creating clear guidelines about what you can and cannot handle during your grief journey. This might involve limiting social interactions, adjusting work responsibilities, or communicating specific needs to those around you.

Learning to communicate these boundaries effectively is crucial for their success. Consider using clear, direct statements that acknowledge others' intentions while firmly expressing your needs. For example, instead of making excuses or apologising repeatedly, try phrases like:

- 'I appreciate your concern, but I need some space right now'
- 'I'm not ready to discuss this yet, but I'll let you know when I am'
- 'Thank you for thinking of me, but I need to decline this invitation'

It's particularly important to establish boundaries around how and when you discuss your loss. You have the right to control your grief narrative and choose when, where, and with whom you share your experience. This might mean preparing simple responses for unexpected questions or having strategies ready for removing yourself from uncomfortable situations.

In professional settings, boundary setting takes on additional importance. Working with your supervisor to establish clear parameters around your needs can help prevent overwhelming situations. This might include:

- Designating a private space for emotional moments
- Creating signals or code words for when you need a break
- Establishing protocols for handling grief related situations
- Setting realistic expectations about your current capacity

Remember that boundaries may need to shift and evolve as your grief journey progresses. What feels necessary and helpful in the early days of loss might change as time passes. Regular check ins with yourself about your boundaries can help ensure they continue to serve your needs effectively.

It's also important to acknowledge that maintaining boundaries can be challenging, especially when faced with resistance or lack of understanding from others. Some people might interpret your boundaries as rejection or take them personally. Having prepared responses and remaining firm in your commitment to self-care can help navigate these challenging interactions.

Protecting your right to grieve also means being mindful of digital boundaries. Social media and constant connectivity can create additional pressure during the grieving process. Consider:
- Adjusting your social media presence or taking breaks when needed
- Setting limits on grief related communications
- Creating boundaries around sharing photos or memories online
- Protecting your privacy while still maintaining meaningful connections

Establishing and maintaining boundaries isn't selfish, it's a necessary part of honouring your grief journey and protecting your healing process. These boundaries create the space you need to process your loss at your own pace, free from external pressures or expectations.

Remember that you have the right to adjust or reinforce your boundaries as needed. Your primary responsibility during grief is to honour your own needs and healing process, even if that means disappointing or disagreeing with others. By protecting your right to grieve in your own way, you create the conditions necessary for authentic healing and growth. As we close this chapter, it's vital to remember that grief's timeline belongs to you alone. Throughout these pages, we've explored how external pressures, and societal expectations can impact our grieving process, yet the most powerful act of self-care is often giving ourselves permission to grieve at our own pace.

The workplace example we discussed demonstrates how creating flexible, personalised approaches to grief can lead to more authentic healing. Whether it's taking private moments during the workday, adjusting responsibilities, or communicating clear boundaries with colleagues, these strategies show that it's possible to honour both our professional commitments and our need to grieve.

The tools and strategies we've explored, from setting healthy boundaries to understanding grief's cycles serve as practical guides for navigating a world that often misunderstands the nature of loss. These approaches aren't about isolating ourselves or rejecting support, but rather about creating the space we need to process our grief authentically.

Remember that resistance to external pressure isn't a sign of weakness or failure to cope it's an act of self-respect and understanding. By acknowledging that grief doesn't follow a prescribed timeline, we free ourselves to experience our emotions honestly and find ways to carry our loss that feel true to our experience.

As you move forward from this chapter, consider that each day might bring unique needs and challenges. Some days you might feel strong enough to engage fully with the world, while others might require more gentle self-care and understanding. Both are equally valid parts of your journey.

Your grief path is uniquely yours, shaped by your relationship with what was lost, your personal history, and your individual needs. The pressure to conform to others' expectations about grief doesn't diminish your right to grieve in your own way, at your own pace. By protecting this right, you create the conditions necessary for genuine healing and growth.

In the chapters ahead, we'll build on these foundations, exploring more ways to honour your unique journey while developing the resilience needed to carry grief in a world that often misunderstands its nature. Remember, there is no universal timeline for healing, only your own authentic path forward.

5. SACRED SPACES: CREATING ROOM FOR PERSONAL HEALING

In the landscape of grief, we often need physical sanctuaries where our hearts can safely unfold their sorrow without judgment or interruption. Creating these sacred spaces whether a quiet corner in your home, a peaceful garden spot, or even a simple ritual space on your desk, can provide essential anchoring points in the stormy seas of loss. Within these sacred spaces, we find permission to experience our grief authentically and fully, without the need to maintain social facades or meet others' expectations. These personal sanctuaries serve as vital anchors in our healing journey, offering refuge when the weight of loss feels particularly heavy.

Creating a dedicated space for grieving isn't about isolating ourselves from life, but rather about establishing intentional environments where we can process our emotions at our own pace. Such spaces might be as elaborate as a transformed room or as simple as a meaningful shelf what matters is that they provide a consistent, safe harbour for our grief experience.

The importance of these spaces became particularly evident in a grief support group, where participants often spoke about feeling overwhelmed by their environments after loss. One member's experience of transforming a small corner of their apartment into a dedicated grief space demonstrated how even modest sanctuaries could provide profound support. They had thoughtfully placed a comfortable chair, meaningful photos, and a journal in their chosen corner, creating an area where they could freely express their emotions.

This space evolved into more than just a physical location, it became a morning companion for coffee with memories, a quiet retreat for evening reflections, and a reliable refuge when grief waves hit unexpectedly during the day. Their example inspired others in the group to create their own sacred spaces, ranging from simple shelves with meaningful objects to transformed spare rooms. These personal sanctuaries became powerful tools for processing grief, offering safe harbours where they could retreat when feeling overwhelmed by the outside world's expectations.

Through these experiences, it became clear that creating intentional spaces for grieving provides both emotional safety and practical support in the healing journey. These sacred spaces offer us permission to be fully present with our loss, to honour our memories, and to process our grief in ways that feel authentic to our individual needs.

As we explore the concept of sacred spaces throughout this chapter, we'll examine practical approaches to creating and maintaining these healing environments. We'll look at how to incorporate meaningful objects and rituals, establish healthy boundaries to protect these spaces, and use them effectively as tools for processing grief. Most importantly, we'll understand how these dedicated areas can help us navigate the complex journey of loss while honouring our need for both solitude and connection.

Designing Physical Sanctuaries: Creating Safe Spaces for Grieving

When creating a physical sanctuary for grieving, the key is to establish an environment that feels both safe and nurturing.

These spaces serve as personal retreats where we can process

our emotions without interruption or judgment. Consider the following elements when designing your grief sanctuary:
- Natural light and fresh air when possible
- Comfortable seating that supports extended periods of reflection
- Meaningful objects that connect to memories and emotions
- Privacy features like curtains or room dividers
- Soft, soothing textures in blankets or cushions
- A journal or creative materials for expression
- Photos or mementos that bring comfort

The physical environment profoundly impacts our emotional processing, which is why thoughtful sanctuary design matters so much during grief. A well designed grief space provides both emotional safety and practical comfort, allowing us to fully experience our feelings without external pressure or interruption.

When selecting a location for your sanctuary, consider both accessibility and privacy. Some may find comfort in transforming a spare room, while others might carve out a corner of their bedroom or create a peaceful spot in their garden. The key is choosing a space you can reliably access when grief waves hit, while ensuring enough privacy to express emotions freely.

Remember that your sanctuary doesn't need to be elaborate or permanent. Even a simple arrangement of meaningful items on a bedside table can serve as a powerful anchor point during difficult moments. What matters most is that the space feels authentic to your needs and provides consistent support for your grieving process.

Consider incorporating elements that engage multiple senses in your sanctuary. A soft blanket for comfort, gentle lighting for atmosphere, perhaps a meaningful scent from a candle or essential oil diffuser. These sensory elements can help ground us when grief feels overwhelming and provide subtle cues that this is a space for processing emotions.

- Avoid cluttering the space with too many items
- Keep electronics and distractions to a minimum
- Choose calming colours and textures
- Include storage for grief related materials
- Consider sound management through soft furnishings

The process of creating your sanctuary can itself be therapeutic. Take time to thoughtfully select each element, considering how it supports your grief journey. Some find comfort in gradually building their space over time, allowing it to evolve as their needs change.

Your grief sanctuary should feel like a gentle invitation rather than another obligation. There's no pressure to use it in any particular way or on any specific schedule. Some days you might spend hours there; other days, just knowing it exists can provide comfort. The space should flex to meet your changing needs while maintaining its core purpose as a safe harbour for your grief experience.

Remember that maintaining boundaries around your sanctuary is essential. This might mean having conversations with family members about respecting the space, establishing quiet hours, or creating simple signals for when you need uninterrupted time there. These boundaries help preserve the sanctuary's role as a reliable refuge during difficult moments.

- Set clear expectations with household members
- Establish simple protocols for using the space
- Create signals for when you need privacy
- Maintain the space's cleanliness and order
- Adjust elements as your needs change

The effectiveness of a grief sanctuary often lies in its consistency and accessibility. Having a dedicated space where you can reliably retreat provides an important sense of control during a time when so much feels beyond our influence. This predictability can help anchor us when grief feels particularly destabilising.

Emotional Boundaries: Protecting Your Healing Environment

Just as physical spaces need protection, our emotional environment requires careful boundaries during grief. These boundaries serve as invisible shields that help us maintain our emotional wellbeing while navigating the complex landscape of loss. Creating and maintaining healthy emotional boundaries becomes especially crucial when we're vulnerable and processing grief.

Emotional boundaries in grief might include limiting exposure to certain social situations, being selective about who we share our grief journey with and feeling empowered to say 'no' to activities or interactions that feel overwhelming. These boundaries aren't walls that keep others out but rather filters that help us manage our emotional energy and protect our healing process.

Consider these essential aspects of emotional boundary setting during grief:

- Permission to decline social invitations without guilt
- Control over how and when to share your grief story
- Freedom to change or cancel plans when grief feels overwhelming
- Authority to limit exposure to potentially triggering situations
- Right to maintain privacy about your grieving process

Setting and maintaining these boundaries often challenges us to prioritise our needs over others' expectations. Many find themselves struggling with guilt when establishing limits, particularly with well-meaning friends and family who want to help. Remember that protecting your emotional space isn't selfish, it's a necessary part of healing.

In grief support settings, participants often discover that clear boundaries actually strengthen relationships rather than damage them. When we communicate our needs honestly and consistently, we create space for more authentic connections with those who truly support our healing journey.

Practical strategies for maintaining emotional boundaries might include preparing simple, direct responses for common situations. For instance, having a prepared phrase like "Thank you for thinking of me, but I need some quiet time right now" can help navigate uncomfortable social pressures while honouring your needs.

Consider these important elements when establishing emotional boundaries:
- Clear communication about your needs and limits
- Consistent application of your boundaries
- Regular reassessment as your needs change
- Respect for others while maintaining your limits
- Support systems that understand and reinforce your boundaries

Remember that emotional boundaries may need to shift and evolve as you move through your grief journey. What feels necessary one month might feel restrictive the next, or vice versa. Give yourself permission to adjust these boundaries as needed, always keeping your emotional wellbeing at the centre of these decisions.

Protecting your emotional environment also means being mindful of digital boundaries in today's connected world. This might involve limiting social media exposure, managing grief related content in your feed, or setting clear expectations about digital communication with friends and family.

When establishing boundaries, it's helpful to identify specific triggers and challenges in your environment. This awareness allows you to create more effective protective measures while remaining open to genuine support and connection. The goal isn't isolation but rather creating a safe emotional space where healing can occur naturally.

Remember that maintaining boundaries requires ongoing

attention and care. Like tending a garden, we must regularly check and adjust our emotional boundaries to ensure they continue serving our healing journey effectively. This might mean having difficult conversations, reinforcing limits when they're tested, or modifying boundaries as our needs evolve.

Ritual and Remembrance: Incorporating Meaningful Objects and Practices

The incorporation of meaningful objects and rituals into our grief journey provides tangible anchors for our memories and emotions. These physical reminders and repeated practices offer comfort while helping us maintain healthy connections with what we've lost. Through intentional rituals and carefully chosen objects, we create bridges between past and present that support our healing journey.

Meaningful objects serve as touchstones that can ground us during overwhelming moments and provide comfort when we need to feel connected to our loss.

Consider these ways to incorporate significant items into your grief journey:
- Keep a small memento in your pocket or bag for difficult days
- Create a memory box with important items and photos
- Display meaningful objects in your sacred space
- Wear or carry something that belonged to your loved one
- Keep a special item on your desk or bedside table

The power of these objects lies not in their monetary value but in their emotional significance and ability to help us maintain connections while processing our grief. Many find that having tangible reminders provides comfort without preventing forward movement in their healing journey.

Rituals play an equally important role in grief processing, offering structure and meaning during times that can feel chaotic and meaningless. These practices don't need to be elaborate or formal simple, consistent actions can provide powerful support for our grieving process.

Consider developing personal rituals that feel authentic to your relationship with loss. This might involve morning coffee with a loved one's photo, lighting a candle on significant dates, or maintaining traditions that hold special meaning. The key is choosing practices that provide comfort and connection rather than obligation or additional stress.

Many find that combining meaningful objects with simple rituals creates particularly powerful healing practices. For instance, writing in a journal kept in your sacred space, or tending to a plant that holds special significance.

These combined practices often provide both emotional comfort and practical coping tools.

- Morning or evening reflection rituals
- Special date remembrance practices
- Nature based ceremonies or activities
- Creative expression rituals
- Memory sharing traditions

When establishing remembrance practices, remember that they should feel supportive rather than burdensome. Start small with simple rituals that you can maintain consistently, allowing them to evolve as your needs change. Some practices might be daily, while others occur only on significant dates or when you feel particularly drawn to them.

It's important to recognise that our relationship with meaningful objects and rituals may shift over time. What provides comfort in early grief might feel different months or years later. Give yourself permission to adapt these practices as needed, always keeping your emotional wellbeing at the centre of these decisions.

Consider how to incorporate meaningful objects and rituals into your daily life in ways that feel natural and sustainable. This might mean keeping a special photo on your desk, wearing a meaningful piece of jewellery, or maintaining a simple morning remembrance practice. The goal is to create touchstones that support your grief journey without overwhelming your daily routine.

Remember that these practices serve as bridges, not barriers. They should help us maintain healthy connections with our loss while supporting our ability to move forward with life. If certain objects or rituals begin to feel heavy or hindering rather than helpful, it's okay to adjust or release them.

When sharing space with others, communicate about your meaningful objects and rituals to ensure they're respected. This might mean explaining why certain items shouldn't be moved or requesting privacy for particular practices. Clear communication helps create understanding and support for these important aspects of your grief journey. As we conclude our exploration of sacred spaces in grief, we're reminded that creating and maintaining these personal sanctuaries isn't just about physical locations it's about honouring our fundamental need for safe harbours in the storm of loss. These spaces, whether elaborate or simple, serve as vital anchors in our healing journey, offering refuge when the weight of grief feels particularly heavy.

Throughout this chapter, we've examined how intentional environments can support our grieving process, from the careful selection of meaningful objects to the establishment of protective boundaries. We've seen how these sacred spaces can evolve alongside our grief, providing consistent support while adapting to our changing needs. The experiences shared in grief support settings have demonstrated the profound impact of having dedicated areas for processing loss, places where we can freely express our emotions without judgment or interruption.

The creation of these sanctuaries reflects a deeper truth about grief: that we need and deserve spaces where our loss can be acknowledged and honoured without pressure to 'move on' or 'get over it.' Whether it's a transformed room, a peaceful garden corner, or simply a meaningful shelf, these spaces validate our ongoing connection with loss while supporting our gradual healing.

As you move forward in your grief journey, remember that

establishing and maintaining these sacred spaces is an act of self-compassion. They serve not as hiding places from life, but as nurturing environments where we can process our grief at our own pace and in our own way. Through these intentional spaces, we create room for both our sorrow and our gradual steps toward healing.

The boundaries we set around these spaces, both physical and emotional help preserve their role as reliable refuges during difficult moments. By protecting these sanctuaries, we honour our need for authentic grieving while maintaining connections with supportive others who respect our journey.

Moving forward, consider how you might create or enhance your own grief sanctuary. Remember that it doesn't need to be elaborate or permanent, what matters most is that it feels authentic to your needs and provides consistent support for your grieving process. Let your sacred space evolve as you do, always serving as a gentle reminder that your grief deserves space, time, and tender care.

6. THE HIDDEN WEIGHT: MANAGING GRIEF IN PROFESSIONAL SPACES

The intersection of grief and professional life creates a unique challenge that many find themselves unprepared to navigate. Behind computer screens, in conference rooms, and throughout office corridors, countless individuals carry the invisible weight of loss while striving to maintain their professional composure. For those navigating loss while maintaining professional responsibilities, this delicate balance can feel like walking a tightrope without a safety net. The workplace often becomes an unexpected battlefield where grief collides with deadlines, meetings, and the pressure to maintain a composed exterior. This chapter explores the complex terrain of managing grief in professional settings, offering practical strategies for both those experiencing loss and those supporting grieving colleagues.

The impact of grief on professional performance is both natural and significant. Common experiences include difficulty concentrating, decreased productivity, memory lapses, and emotional overwhelm. These responses aren't signs of weakness or unprofessionalism they're normal symptoms of grief that deserve understanding and accommodation.

During a management training session focused on supporting grieving employees, a leader shared their experience of leading a team member through loss. The team member had recently lost their parent and was struggling to maintain their usual high performance standards. Instead of pushing for immediate productivity, the supervisor worked with HR to implement flexible working arrangements and created a supportive environment where the employee could step away when grief waves hit. They established clear communication channels and adjusted project timelines thoughtfully. This approach not only helped the grieving employee maintain their professional role while processing their loss but also fostered a more compassionate workplace culture. The team's response demonstrated how professional spaces can accommodate grief while maintaining productivity, showing that empathy and efficiency aren't mutually exclusive. This experience transformed the department's approach to supporting grieving colleagues, leading to the development of more comprehensive grief support policies.

This story illustrates a fundamental truth about grief in the workplace: when organisations create space for authentic grieving while maintaining appropriate professional boundaries, both the individual and the organisation benefit. It's not about choosing between supporting a grieving employee and maintaining productivity, it's about finding ways to do both effectively.

As we explore this chapter, we'll examine practical strategies for managing grief at work, communicating needs to employers and colleagues, and creating supportive professional environments that acknowledge the reality of loss while maintaining necessary business functions. Whether you're personally navigating grief in your professional life or supporting others through their journey, understanding these dynamics is crucial for creating workplaces that honour both human experience and professional responsibility.

Professional Boundaries: Balancing Emotional Needs with Workplace Expectations

Setting and maintaining professional boundaries while grieving requires a delicate balance between honouring your emotional needs and meeting workplace responsibilities. These boundaries serve as essential guidelines that protect both your healing process and your professional relationships.

Key aspects of maintaining healthy professional boundaries include:
- Deciding how much personal information to share with colleagues
- Establishing clear communication channels with supervisors about needs and limitations
- Creating strategies for managing unexpected emotional moments at work
- Setting realistic expectations for productivity and performance
- Developing plans for handling grief triggers in professional settings

When establishing these boundaries, it's crucial to remember that they may need regular adjustment as your grief journey evolves. What works in the initial stages of loss might need modification as you move through different phases of grieving.

One effective approach is to develop a personal toolkit for managing grief at work. This might include identifying a private space where you can take brief breaks when emotions feel overwhelming, keeping grounding objects at your desk, or establishing signal phrases with trusted colleagues when you need support or space.

For managers and supervisors, supporting grieving employees while maintaining professional boundaries involves:
- Creating clear policies about bereavement leave and flexible work arrangements
- Establishing consistent check in protocols that respect

privacy
- Developing support systems that maintain professional dynamics
- Setting appropriate expectations for team communication and project management

It's equally important to recognise signs when professional boundaries need strengthening. These might include feeling overwhelmed by colleagues' questions about your loss, difficulty maintaining work life separation, or experiencing increased emotional exhaustion at work.

Practical strategies for reinforcing professional boundaries while grieving include:
- Preparing brief, professional responses to common questions about your loss
- Scheduling regular breaks throughout the workday for emotional processing
- Creating transition rituals between work and personal time
- Establishing clear parameters for workplace accommodations
- Maintaining consistent professional communication patterns

Remember that setting boundaries isn't about building walls, it's about creating necessary structure that allows you to honour both your grief journey and your professional commitments. These boundaries protect your emotional wellbeing while ensuring you can continue to function effectively in your professional role.

It's also vital to recognise when existing boundaries need adjustment. Signs that boundaries may need strengthening include feeling emotionally depleted after work interactions, struggling to maintain professional composure, or experiencing increased anxiety about workplace situations.

Effective boundary setting includes being clear about your needs while remaining professional. For example, rather than avoiding work social events entirely, you might choose to attend for a limited time or select specific events that feel manageable. This approach allows you to maintain professional connections while protecting your emotional energy.

When communicating boundaries, use clear, professional language that focuses on solutions rather than explanations. Instead of detailed explanations about your emotional state, simple statements like "I need to step away for a moment" or "I'll need to adjust my schedule for this project" can be effective while maintaining professional dignity.

Communication Strategies: Discussing Grief with Employers and Colleagues

One of the most challenging aspects of navigating grief in the workplace is communicating effectively about your experience and needs. Clear, professional communication can help create understanding and establish necessary support systems while maintaining appropriate workplace boundaries.

When approaching conversations about grief with employers and colleagues, consider these essential strategies:

- Schedule private conversations with supervisors to discuss your situation
- Prepare key points about necessary accommodations or support needed
- Focus on specific, practical impacts rather than emotional details
- Establish preferred communication methods for ongoing updates
- Define clear parameters around information sharing with wider team

The timing and depth of these conversations matter significantly. While immediate supervisors need to be informed about your situation, you can be more selective about what you share with colleagues. Consider preparing a brief, professional response for common questions or expressions of condolence.

When communicating with your employer, focus on concrete impacts and solutions rather than emotional details. For example, instead of sharing the emotional toll of your loss, discuss specific needs like flexible scheduling for grief counselling appointments or temporary adjustments to workload. This approach maintains professional boundaries while ensuring necessary support.

For managers and colleagues supporting someone through grief, effective communication includes:

- Respecting privacy and confidentiality
- Following the grieving person's lead on discussion topics
- Avoiding unsolicited advice or personal grief stories
- Maintaining consistent but unobtrusive check ins
- Focusing on practical support rather than emotional counsel

It's important to establish clear channels for ongoing communication about changing needs or challenges. Regular check ins with supervisors can help address emerging issues before they become overwhelming, while maintaining professional dynamics.

When grief impacts your work performance, transparent communication becomes crucial.

Rather than struggling silently, consider proactively discussing temporary accommodations or support needs. This might include:
- Requesting temporary deadline adjustments
- Discussing flexible work arrangements
- Establishing backup support for critical tasks
- Creating signal systems for difficult moments
- Setting clear expectations for communication availability

Remember that workplace communication about grief should remain professional while being authentic. You don't need to share every detail of your experience, but acknowledging its impact on your work life can help create understanding and necessary support structures.

For team environments, consider working with HR or your supervisor to establish guidelines for communicating your situation to colleagues. This can help manage well-meaning but potentially overwhelming expressions of support while maintaining professional boundaries.

Effective communication also includes being clear about your preferences for how others acknowledge your loss. Some may prefer minimal acknowledgment at work, while others might appreciate occasional check ins. Whatever your preference, communicating clearly can help colleagues provide appropriate support.

When emotions arise at work, having predetermined strategies for communication can be invaluable. This might include having prepared phrases for excusing yourself from situations, established signals with supportive colleagues, or designated spaces for brief recovery periods.

Remember that your communication needs may change as you move through different phases of grief. Regular reassessment of these strategies ensures they continue to serve both your healing process and professional responsibilities effectively.

Workplace Support Systems: Creating and Accessing Professional Grief Resources

Creating robust workplace support systems for grieving employees is essential for both individual wellbeing and organisational health. These systems provide structured assistance while acknowledging the complex nature of grief in professional settings.

Effective workplace support systems typically include:
- Employee Assistance Programs (EAP) offering confidential counselling services
- Flexible bereavement leave policies that acknowledge several types of loss
- Clear procedures for requesting and accessing grief support resources
- Training programs for managers on supporting grieving team members
- Peer support networks or grief support groups

When implementing these support systems, organisations should focus on accessibility and confidentiality. Employees need to know not only what resources are available but also how to access them discreetly when needed. This might include having information readily available through internal websites, employee handbooks, or dedicated resource coordinators.

For managers and HR professionals, creating effective support systems involves establishing clear protocols while maintaining flexibility to accommodate individual needs.

This includes developing guidelines for:
- Documenting and communicating available support resources
- Training supervisors in grief sensitive management practices
- Creating return to work transition plans
- Establishing accommodation request procedures
- Maintaining confidentiality while coordinating support

The effectiveness of workplace support systems often depends on how well they're integrated into the organisation's culture. When support resources are treated as a normal and expected part of workplace infrastructure, employees are more likely to utilise them when needed.

Practical steps for accessing professional grief resources in the workplace include:
- Reviewing employee benefits documentation for available support services
- Connecting with HR representatives about specific grief support options
- Exploring EAP services for counselling and resource referrals
- Investigating workplace support groups or peer counselling programs
- Understanding bereavement leave policies and flexibility options

It's crucial to remember that accessing support resources isn't a sign of professional weakness but rather a demonstration of self-awareness and responsibility. Organisations that normalise the use of grief support services often see better outcomes in terms of employee retention and long-term productivity.

For organisations looking to enhance their grief support systems, consider:
- Regular reviews and updates of bereavement policies
- Feedback mechanisms for improving support services
- Partnerships with external grief support organisations
- Development of resource libraries and information packets
- Creation of quiet spaces or reflection rooms

Effective workplace support systems acknowledge that grief impacts extend beyond immediate bereavement. Long term support options might include:
- Ongoing counselling services through EAP programs
- Flexible work arrangements during significant grief anniversaries
- Regular check ins with supervisors or HR representatives
- Access to grief education resources and workshops
- Connection with peer support networks

Remember that workplace support systems should be designed to accommodate different grieving styles and needs. What works for one employee may not work for another, making flexibility and variety in support options essential.

When developing or accessing these resources, maintain clear professional boundaries while ensuring support remains accessible. This might mean creating structured ways to request assistance or establishing specific channels for communicating needs related to grief.

The success of workplace grief support systems often lies in their ability to balance structure with flexibility, providing clear access to resources while allowing for personalised support approaches. Regular evaluation and adjustment of these systems ensures they continue to meet the evolving needs of grieving employees while maintaining professional standards. As we conclude this chapter on managing grief in professional spaces, it's essential to recognise that the workplace often serves as a microcosm where our personal and professional lives intersect in profound ways. The strategies and insights shared throughout this chapter demonstrate that creating supportive professional environments while maintaining appropriate boundaries isn't just compassionate it's good business practice.

The intersection of grief and work life presents unique challenges that require thoughtful navigation. We've explored how establishing clear communication channels, setting appropriate boundaries, and accessing workplace support systems can create a foundation for managing grief while maintaining professional responsibilities. These tools become especially vital when we consider that most adults spend a significant portion of their waking hours at work, making it impossible to completely separate our grief experience from our professional lives.

The workplace support examples we've examined show that effective grief support doesn't compromise professional standard. Instead, it enhances them by acknowledging our shared humanity. When organisations implement flexible policies, provide clear support resources, and train managers in grief sensitive leadership, they create environments where both productivity and healing can coexist.

Perhaps most importantly, we've learned that managing grief in professional spaces isn't about hiding or minimising our experiences, but rather about finding appropriate ways to acknowledge and work with them. Whether you're personally navigating loss while maintaining professional responsibilities or supporting grieving colleagues, remember that creating space for grief in the workplace doesn't diminish professional capability it acknowledges the full spectrum of human experience that exists in every workplace.

As you move forward, consider how the strategies discussed in this chapter might be adapted to your specific workplace situation. Remember that managing grief at work is an ongoing process that may require regular adjustment of boundaries, communication approaches, and support needs. Trust that by acknowledging and appropriately accommodating grief in professional spaces, we create workplaces that are not only more compassionate but ultimately more effective.

In the next chapter, we'll explore how to support others through their grief journey, building on many of the communication and boundary setting skills we've discussed here. Whether you're a colleague, supervisor, or friend, understanding how to provide compassionate support while respecting appropriate boundaries is crucial for creating healing connections.

7. COMPASSIONATE SUPPORT: GUIDING OTHERS THROUGH LOSS

Supporting someone through grief requires a delicate balance of presence and patience, where our role is not to fix their pain but to walk beside them as they navigate their loss. The most profound support often comes not from having the right words, but from having the courage to sit with someone in their darkness, holding space for their grief without trying to brighten it. When we witness someone navigating the depths of grief, our instinct often pulls us toward trying to fix their pain or fill the silence with well-meaning platitudes. Yet, as many discover through their own experiences of loss, true support requires a different approach, one that embraces the art of presence over the impulse to solve.

Compassionate support begins with understanding that grief manifests differently for each person, influenced by their unique relationship with what was lost, their cultural background, and their personal coping style. While one person might need space for quiet reflection, another might seek active engagement in shared memories. The key lies not in prescribing a particular path but in remaining flexible and attentive to each person's individual needs.

The challenge of supporting others through grief becomes particularly evident in the story shared during a grief support training session. The participant's journey from offering quick fixes and spiritual platitudes to learning the power of simple presence illustrates a fundamental truth about grief support sometimes the most profound help we can offer is our willingness to sit with someone in their darkness, without trying to illuminate it prematurely.

This shift from 'fixing' to 'being present' represents a crucial evolution in how we approach grief support. It acknowledges that grief isn't a problem to be solved but rather an experience to be witnessed and honoured. The simple act of asking 'What do you need right now?' opens space for authentic expression and validates the griever's authority over their own journey.

Practical support plays an equally vital role, though it too requires mindful consideration. The bringing of meals, helping with errands, or simply maintaining regular contact demonstrates commitment to walking alongside someone through their grief journey. These tangible expressions of care become particularly meaningful in the weeks and months after the initial wave of support has passed, when many grieving individuals find themselves facing the ongoing reality of their loss in a world that appears to have moved on.

As we explore the various dimensions of providing compassionate support, this chapter will offer practical guidance for being present with others in their grief while maintaining healthy boundaries. We'll examine common pitfalls to avoid, discuss ways to sustain support over time, and explore how to create safe spaces for authentic grieving. Through understanding these principles, we can become more effective companions to those navigating the complex terrain of loss.

Active Listening: The Art of Being Present Without Trying to Fix
Active listening emerges as one of the most powerful tools we can offer someone experiencing grief, yet it's often one of the most

challenging skills to master. In our natural desire to ease another's pain, we frequently rush to fill silence with advice or attempt to redirect their thoughts toward more positive territory. However, true active listening requires us to resist these impulses and instead create space for authentic expression of grief.

The foundation of active listening in grief support rests on three key principles: focused attention, non-judgment, and emotional presence. When someone shares their grief experience, our role is to listen with our full being not just our ears, but with our body language, facial expressions, and most importantly, with our heart. This means setting aside our own discomfort with their pain and resisting the urge to offer solutions or comparisons to other grief experiences.

- Maintain eye contact when culturally appropriate
- Use gentle nodding or subtle expressions to show engagement
- Allow for comfortable silence without rushing to fill it
- Keep your body language open and relaxed
- Avoid checking phones or watches during conversations

When someone shares their grief, our responses can either open or close doors to deeper connection. Simple acknowledgments like 'That sounds incredibly difficult' or 'I hear how much pain you're in' validate their experience without trying to change it. These responses create safe spaces where all emotions anger, confusion, sadness, or even moments of unexpected joy can exist without judgment.

The art of being present also involves recognising and managing our own emotional responses. When we witness someone's grief, it often stirs our own experiences of loss or triggers our helping instincts. Learning to sit with these feelings without acting on them becomes crucial for maintaining the focus on the grieving person's needs rather than our own need to fix or comfort.

- Avoid phrases that minimise grief like 'At least they're no longer suffering'

- Refrain from sharing similar experiences unless specifically asked
- Don't offer unsolicited advice or spiritual perspectives
- Never rush to find silver linings or positive aspects of the loss
- Resist the urge to problem solve unless directly requested

Creating a container for grief means allowing space for repetition. Often, grieving individuals need to tell their story multiple times as part of their processing. Active listening means being willing to hear these stories with the same attention and compassion each time, recognising that each retelling may reveal new aspects of their experience or help them integrate their loss differently.

The power of active listening extends beyond the immediate conversation. When we truly listen, we communicate that the grieving person's experience matters, that their pain is valid, and that they don't need to rush through or minimise their grief to make others comfortable. This validation can become a crucial support in a society that often pressures people to 'move on' quickly from loss.

Remember that active listening doesn't require special training or expertise, it simply requires our authentic presence and willingness to witness another's pain without trying to fix it. Sometimes the most powerful support we can offer is our quiet attention, creating space where grief can be expressed freely and without judgment. This practice of presence becomes particularly valuable in professional settings, where colleagues may feel pressure to 'keep it together' or return to normal functioning quickly after a loss.

Practical Support: Understanding When and How to Offer Tangible Help

While emotional support forms the foundation of grief companionship, practical assistance often provides essential scaffolding for those navigating loss. Understanding when and how to offer tangible help requires both sensitivity to timing and awareness of what truly serves the grieving person's needs. The key lies in offering specific, concrete support rather than vague statements like 'Let me know if you need anything.'

- Offer specific tasks rather than general help
- Coordinate with others to ensure consistent support
- Respect boundaries and preferences around assistance
- Follow through on commitments made
- Be mindful of timing and energy levels

Practical support often proves most valuable when addressing basic needs that may feel overwhelming during intense grief. Simple tasks like preparing meals, managing household chores, or managing administrative duties can provide crucial relief when someone's emotional and physical energy is depleted. However, the manner of offering this support matters as much as the support itself.

When providing practical assistance, it's essential to respect the grieving person's autonomy and preferences. Some may welcome regular meal deliveries, while others might prefer gift cards to local restaurants. Similarly, while one person might appreciate help organising paperwork, another might find such assistance intrusive. The key is to offer choices and remain flexible in your approach.

Timing plays a crucial role in practical support. While many people rally around someone immediately after a loss, the need for tangible help often extends well beyond the initial period of grief. Consider creating a schedule with others to ensure sustained support over time, particularly around significant dates or anniversaries that might trigger stronger grief responses.

- Assist with daily tasks like grocery shopping or lawn care
- Help manage administrative tasks and paperwork
- Provide childcare or pet care when needed
- Offer to drive to appointments or run errands
- Create reminders for important dates and deadlines

In professional settings, practical support might take the form of adjusting workloads, providing flexible scheduling options, or helping to manage communication with clients or colleagues. Managers and colleagues can demonstrate support by offering clear, concrete assistance while respecting professional boundaries and the grieving person's privacy preferences.

When offering practical help, it's important to recognise that grief can affect decision making and energy levels in unpredictable ways. What feels manageable one day might become overwhelming the next. Therefore, maintaining open communication about needs and boundaries becomes essential for providing effective support.

Remember that practical support serves not just to complete tasks, but to create space for grieving. When basic needs are met and daily responsibilities are shared, the grieving person gains more capacity to process their loss and engage in necessary emotional work. This understanding helps guide how we offer and provide tangible assistance.

The coordination of practical support often benefits from clear organisation. Consider using online calendars or meal train websites to coordinate multiple helpers, ensuring support remains consistent without becoming overwhelming. These tools can help prevent duplicate efforts while ensuring no essential needs fall through the cracks.

- Use digital tools to coordinate support efforts
- Maintain consistent communication about changing needs
- Be prepared to adjust support as circumstances change
- Remember that practical needs may evolve over time
- Stay attentive to signs of overwhelm or withdrawal

Effective practical support also involves knowing when to step back or modify assistance. Pay attention to cues that might indicate your help is becoming intrusive or that the grieving person needs more space. Sometimes, the most supportive action is to remain available while allowing them to reclaim independence in certain areas.

Long Term Support: Maintaining Connection Beyond the Initial Crisis

One of the most challenging aspects of grief support lies in maintaining meaningful connection long after the initial crisis has passed. While many people rally around someone in the immediate aftermath of loss, this support often dwindles as time progresses, leaving grieving individuals to navigate their ongoing journey with diminished support when they may need it most.

The reality of long-term grief support requires understanding that grief doesn't follow a linear timeline or conform to societal expectations of 'getting over it.' Significant dates, milestones, and seemingly ordinary moments can trigger grief waves months or years after a loss, making continued support crucial for healing.

- Mark important dates and anniversaries on your calendar
- Schedule regular check ins without waiting for signs of distress
- Maintain consistent contact through various channels (calls, texts, visits)
- Remember to acknowledge holidays and special occasions
- Continue including them in social plans while respecting their choices

Long term support involves recognising that grief evolves rather than ends. What someone needs six months after a loss may differ significantly from their needs during the initial weeks, yet these later stage needs remain equally valid and important. This understanding helps shape how we maintain connection over time.

One of the most valuable aspects of sustained support is the willingness to continue speaking the name of the person who died or acknowledging the loss that occurred. Many grieving individuals express fear that others will forget their loved one or expect them to stop mentioning their loss. By maintaining open dialogue about their grief experience, we validate its ongoing nature and provide crucial emotional support.

- Share memories of the person who died when appropriate
- Listen without judgment when they need to discuss their loss
- Avoid phrases like 'Isn't it time to move on?' or 'Are you still grieving?'
- Recognise that grief may resurface during life transitions
- Maintain awareness of grief triggers and anniversary reactions

In professional settings, long term support might involve continued flexibility with deadlines, understanding about occasional emotional days, and maintaining open communication about changing needs. Managers can demonstrate sustained support by scheduling regular check ins and remaining attentive to signs that additional accommodation might be needed.

The practice of long-term support also involves understanding that grief can be recurring rather than linear. Special occasions, holidays, or even changes in seasons can trigger renewed grief responses. Maintaining awareness of these patterns helps supporters provide more timely and appropriate assistance.

- Be prepared for grief to resurface during significant life events
- Offer extra support during holiday seasons or anniversaries
- Maintain consistency in your support while respecting boundaries
- Remember that healing doesn't mean forgetting
- Stay attuned to changes in their support needs over time

Effective long-term support requires balancing consistent presence with respect for independence. While maintaining connection remains important, supporters must also recognise when to step back and allow space for the grieving person to develop their own coping strategies and rebuild their life at their own pace.

Remember that long term support doesn't always mean grand gestures or intense emotional conversations. Sometimes the most meaningful support comes through simple acknowledgments, a text message on a difficult date, including them in regular activities, or simply showing that you remember and care about their ongoing journey with grief.   The journey of supporting others through grief requires both intentional presence and practical wisdom. As we've explored throughout this chapter, effective support extends far beyond well-meaning platitudes or attempts to fix another's pain. Instead, it calls for the courage to walk alongside others in their darkness, offering both emotional presence and tangible assistance when needed.

The power of active listening has emerged as a cornerstone of compassionate support. By creating space for others to express their grief authentically, without judgment or pressure to 'feel better,' we validate their unique experience and honour the depth of their loss. This practice of presence of truly hearing and witnessing another's pain, can provide crucial support in a society that often rushes to minimise or avoid grief's complexities.

Practical support, when offered mindfully and specifically, provides essential scaffolding for those navigating loss. Whether coordinating meal deliveries, managing administrative tasks, or maintaining regular check ins, these tangible expressions of care demonstrate commitment to supporting others through both immediate crisis and long-term adjustment. The key lies in remaining attentive to changing needs while respecting individual preferences and boundaries.

The importance of sustained support cannot be overstated, particularly as initial waves of assistance naturally fade. By maintaining consistent connection, marking significant dates, and remaining open to ongoing conversations about loss, we help create an environment where authentic grieving can unfold naturally. This long-term perspective acknowledges that grief doesn't follow a predetermined timeline but rather evolves as part of the human experience.

In professional settings, the principles of compassionate support take on additional significance. Managers and colleagues can create more supportive workplace cultures by implementing flexible policies, maintaining open communication, and recognising that grief affects each person differently. This understanding helps bridge the gap between professional expectations and personal healing needs.

Perhaps most importantly, this chapter has emphasised that supporting others through grief doesn't require special expertise or perfect words. Rather, it calls for authentic presence, practical assistance, and the willingness to witness another's pain without trying to fix it. Through these practices, we can create more compassionate communities where grief is acknowledged, supported, and understood as a natural part of the human experience.

As we move forward in our own journeys of supporting others through loss, may we carry these principles with us: the power of presence over platitudes, the importance of practical support offered mindfully, and the ongoing nature of grief that deserves sustained acknowledgment and care. In doing so, we contribute to a culture that better understands and supports the complex nature of grief and loss.

8. HONOURING LOSS: MEANINGFUL WAYS TO REMEMBER AND CONNECT

The act of remembering those we've lost isn't about clinging to the past, but rather about weaving their legacy meaningfully into our present and future. Through intentional practices of remembrance, we can honour our connections while gradually building new meaning in life after loss. In a world that often rushes past pain, taking time to honour our losses creates essential touchstones for healing. These moments of remembrance serve as bridges between past and present, allowing us to maintain meaningful connections while gradually moving forward in our changed lives.

Remembrance takes many forms, each as unique as the grief journey itself. For some, it manifests in quiet rituals, lighting a candle, visiting a special place, or maintaining traditions that hold precious memories. For others, remembrance finds expression through creative outlets or community service, transforming grief into actions that honour both the loss and the love that remains.

During a grief support workshop, this diversity of remembrance practices became beautifully apparent. One participant shared their experience with memorial gardening a practice that proved transformative in their healing journey. Through tending to their loved one's favourite flowers, they discovered a powerful metaphor for grief itself: the cyclical nature of growth, the patience required for nurturing, and the way beauty can emerge from profound loss. The garden became more than a memorial; it evolved into a living testament to love's endurance and the possibility of finding renewal while honouring grief.

Their story illustrates how personal and unique remembrance practices can be, teaching us that there's no 'right' way to maintain connections with what we've lost. Some find comfort in traditional ceremonies, while others create entirely new rituals that feel more authentic to their experience. What matters isn't the form these practices take, but rather how they help us process our grief and maintain meaningful connections.

As we explore various ways to honour loss, remember that these practices aren't about clinging to the past or refusing to move forward. Instead, they're about creating intentional spaces where our love and grief can coexist with our continued growth. Through thoughtful remembrance, we learn to carry our losses not as burdens that weigh us down, but as precious parts of who we are becoming.

This chapter will explore different approaches to remembrance and help you discover practices that resonate with your personal journey. We'll examine how creating meaningful rituals, developing legacy projects, and sharing memories within supportive communities can all contribute to healing while honouring the enduring impact of our losses.

Creating Personal Rituals: Developing Meaningful Ways to Remember

Creating personal rituals provides a structured way to honour our losses while nurturing ongoing connections that support healing. These rituals can range from simple daily practices to more elaborate ceremonies, each serving as an anchor point in our grief journey. The key is finding rituals that feel authentic and meaningful to your personal experience of loss.

Here are some ways to develop meaningful remembrance rituals:
- Morning reflection practices with photos or meaningful objects
- Creating seasonal traditions that honour special dates
- Maintaining connections through favourite activities or places
- Writing letters or keeping a dialogue journal
- Crafting memory boxes or albums
- Preparing favourite meals or recipes

The power of personal rituals lies not in their complexity but in their ability to create intentional moments for processing grief and maintaining connections. These practices provide structure during times when grief feels overwhelming, offering gentle routines that acknowledge both our loss and our need to move forward.

One support group participant found solace in a simple morning ritual of having coffee in their loved one's favourite mug while looking through old photos. This quiet practice became a daily touchstone, providing both comfort and connection. Over time, what began as a grief ritual evolved into a cherished way of starting each day, demonstrating how remembrance practices can become meaningful parts of our new normal.

When developing personal rituals, consider these guiding principles:
- Choose practices that feel natural and sustainable
- Allow rituals to evolve as your needs change
- Include sensory elements that support memory and connection
- Create flexibility for both private and shared remembrance
- Honour both joyful and difficult memories

Remembrance rituals don't need to be sombre or formal. They can incorporate elements of celebration, creativity, and even humour when appropriate. The key is finding ways to acknowledge your loss while nurturing your ongoing relationship with what or whom you've lost.

Many find that combining practical activities with remembrance adds depth to their rituals. For instance, gardening while listening to favourite music, cooking meaningful recipes while sharing stories, or walking in special places while reflecting on memories. These integrated practices help weave remembrance naturally into daily life.

It's important to recognise that rituals may need to adapt over time. What provides comfort in early grief might feel different months or years later. Give yourself permission to modify or create new rituals as your relationship with grief evolves. Some find that certain anniversaries or holidays call for special rituals, while others prefer daily practices that provide regular touchstones for remembrance.

When creating rituals, consider involving others who shared your loss. Collective remembrance practices can strengthen support networks and create spaces for shared healing. However, also maintain personal rituals that honour your individual need for private reflection and connection.

Remember that rituals serve multiple purposes in grief:
- Creating structure during chaotic emotions
- Maintaining healthy connections with what's been lost
- Providing comfort through familiar practices
- Offering ways to express grief physically
- Building new traditions that honour both past and present

Through thoughtful ritual creation, we develop meaningful ways to carry our losses while continuing to engage with life. These practices become bridges between our grief and growth, helping us navigate the delicate balance of remembering and living forward.

Legacy Projects: Honouring Loss Through Creative Expression

Legacy projects offer a powerful way to channel grief into meaningful creative expression while honouring the memory of those we've lost. These projects can take many forms, from artistic endeavours to community initiatives, each serving as a bridge between our past connections and future meaning making. Through creative expression, we find ways to transform our pain into purpose while maintaining lasting connections with our loved ones.

Here are some meaningful ways to develop legacy projects:
- Creating memory books or digital archives of stories and photos
- Starting community initiatives that reflect values or passions
- Developing art projects inspired by shared memories
- Writing poetry, music, or narratives that honour the relationship
- Establishing scholarship funds or charitable programs

The beauty of legacy projects lies in their ability to combine remembrance with forward movement. They provide tangible ways to honour our losses while creating something meaningful that can benefit others or serve as lasting tributes.

In a grief support meeting, one participant found healing through establishing a community garden project. What began as a personal memorial evolved into a neighbourhood gathering space where others could find peace and connection. The project helped them channel their grief into creating something beautiful while honouring their loved one's passion for bringing people together.

When considering a legacy project, focus on initiatives that feel authentic to your relationship and personal experience. The most meaningful projects often emerge from genuine connections to shared values, interests, or dreams. They don't need to be grand gestures sometimes the most powerful tributes come from simple, heartfelt expressions.

Consider these aspects when developing your legacy project:

- Choose projects that feel sustainable and manageable
- Allow room for the project to evolve over time
- Include elements that feel personally meaningful
- Consider ways to involve others if appropriate
- Focus on quality over quantity

Legacy projects can also provide structure during the chaos of grief, offering concrete tasks and goals when other aspects of life feel overwhelming. They create opportunities for active remembrance while building something new, helping us navigate the delicate balance between honouring our past and creating our future.

One particularly healing aspect of legacy projects is their ability to transform private grief into public good. Whether through charitable initiatives, educational programs, or creative works that touch others, these projects can help us find meaning in loss while contributing positively to our communities.

It's important to remember that legacy projects don't need to be completed quickly or perfectly. Like grief itself, they can evolve over time, changing shape as our needs and relationship with loss shift. Some find that working on their project provides comfort during difficult days, while others prefer to engage with it during periods of greater emotional strength.

Consider documenting your legacy project journey, whether through photos, journals, or digital media. This documentation can become part of the legacy itself, capturing not just the final result but the meaningful process of creating something born from love and loss.

Remember these key principles when developing legacy projects:
- Start small and allow room for growth
- Focus on projects that energise rather than drain you
- Include elements that can be shared with others
- Create space for both celebration and remembrance
- Allow the project to evolve with your grief journey

Through thoughtful legacy projects, we create lasting tributes that honour both our losses and our continued growth. These creative expressions become touchstones in our grief journey, helping us maintain meaningful connections while building something new from our experience of loss.

Collective Remembrance: Sharing Memories and Building Community

While personal remembrance practices form an essential part of our grief journey, there's profound healing power in coming together with others to share memories and honour our losses collectively. Community remembrance creates spaces where grief can be witnessed, stories can be shared, and connections can be strengthened through shared understanding.

Collective remembrance serves multiple purposes in the healing journey:
- Creating safe spaces for authentic grief expression
- Building supportive networks with others who understand
- Preserving and sharing important memories
- Reducing isolation common in grief
- Validating diverse grief experiences

When we share our memories in community settings, we often discover new dimensions of our loved ones through others' perspectives. These shared remembrances can help us maintain more complete pictures of those we've lost while fostering connections with others who knew them.

A grief support group demonstrated this beautifully when members began sharing memories of their loved ones' favourite music. What started as simple story sharing evolved into a monthly gathering where participants would play meaningful songs and share the stories behind them. These sessions created profound connections while helping everyone maintain vibrant memories of their loved ones through different perspectives.

Creating collective remembrance opportunities doesn't require formal settings or large groups.

Consider these accessible ways to build community around shared memories:
- Memory sharing circles with family or close friends
- Collaborative memory books or digital archives
- Group activities honouring shared connections
- Community service projects in memory of loved ones
- Regular gatherings on significant dates

The key to successful collective remembrance lies in creating environments where all expressions of grief are welcomed and validated. These spaces should feel safe for sharing both joyful and difficult memories, allowing authentic expression without judgment.

One particularly meaningful approach involves creating regular opportunities for shared remembrance through simple activities. A neighbourhood walking group formed by several grieving individuals found that their weekly walks naturally evolved into times of memory sharing. The combination of gentle movement and casual conversation created an environment where stories could emerge organically, without pressure or formality.

When organising collective remembrance activities, consider these important factors:
- Ensure everyone feels welcome to participate at their comfort level
- Create structure while allowing for natural conversation flow
- Respect different grieving styles and expression needs
- Maintain consistent gathering times when possible
- Allow space for both tears and laughter

Remember that collective remembrance doesn't mean everyone needs to share the same type of loss or grief experience. Often, the most supportive communities form around shared understanding of grief itself, rather than identical circumstances.

Building community through shared remembrance also helps challenge the isolation that often accompanies grief in our society. When we come together to honour our losses, we create counter cultural spaces where ongoing grief is normalised and supported rather than rushed or dismissed.

Consider these guidelines for fostering supportive remembrance communities:

- Establish basic ground rules about respect and confidentiality
- Create predictable structures while remaining flexible
- Welcome new members while maintaining group cohesion
- Balance sharing time among participants
- Honour both presence and absence as needed

Through thoughtful collective remembrance practices, we build communities that support both individual and shared healing. These connections remind us that while grief may be uniquely personal, we need not walk its path alone. By creating spaces where memories can be shared and honoured together, we strengthen our capacity to carry our losses while supporting others in their journey.

Remember that participating in collective remembrance doesn't require constant attendance or sharing. Some may find comfort simply being present while others share, while some may need to step in and out of community spaces as their energy and needs fluctuate. The key is creating accessible opportunities for connection while respecting individual boundaries and needs. As we conclude this chapter on honouring loss through remembrance, we recognise that finding meaningful ways to remember and connect is not about staying anchored in the past, but rather about weaving our loved ones' legacies into our ongoing journey. Through personal rituals, legacy projects, and collective remembrance, we discover that honouring loss can take many forms, each as unique as our individual grief experience.

The practices and approaches we've explored from memorial gardens to community gatherings, from simple daily rituals to lasting legacy projects demonstrate that there is no single 'right' way to remember. What matters most is finding methods that feel authentic to your relationship with loss and sustainable for your healing journey.

Remembrance serves as a bridge between our past and present, allowing us to maintain meaningful connections while gradually building new lives around our losses. Through intentional practices of memory keeping, we learn that moving forward doesn't mean leaving our loved ones behind. Instead, we find ways to carry them with us, allowing their influence to continue shaping our lives in positive ways.

The stories shared throughout this chapter illustrate how remembrance practices often evolve over time, changing shape as our relationship with grief shifts and grows. What begins as a private ritual may blossom into a community project; what starts as a simple tribute might develop into a lasting legacy. These transformations remind us that honouring loss is not a static practice but a dynamic journey that grows with us.

As you consider your own path forward, remember that there's no timeline for establishing remembrance practices. Some may find comfort in creating rituals immediately, while others need time before feeling ready to engage in formal remembrance. Trust your instincts about what feels right for you, knowing that these practices can be adjusted or reimagined as your needs change.

Perhaps most importantly, this chapter reminds us that remembrance can coexist with healing, that honouring our losses doesn't prevent us from building meaningful lives after loss. Through thoughtful practices of remembrance, we create space for both our grief and our growth, our memories and our future hopes.

As you move forward from this chapter, consider starting small with remembrance practices that feel manageable and meaningful to you. Allow yourself to experiment with different approaches, knowing that what works for others may not work for you, and what works for you today may need adjustment tomorrow. Remember that the goal isn't to create perfect tributes or unchanging rituals, but rather to find ways of honouring your loss that support your healing journey while maintaining meaningful connections to those you've lost.

In the end, remembrance is not about holding onto pain, but about transforming our love into lasting legacies that enrich our lives and often touch others as well. Through mindful practices of remembrance, we learn that it's possible to honour our losses while continuing to grow, to remember while moving forward, and to carry our loved ones with us as we build new meaning in life after loss.

9. BUILDING RESILIENCE: GENTLE STEPS TOWARD HEALING

Resilience in grief isn't about bouncing back to who we were before loss but about growing our capacity to carry our grief while gradually rebuilding our lives. Like a garden that slowly recovers after a storm, our healing journey involves gentle nurturing, patience, and an understanding that new growth doesn't erase what was lost but rather creates space for both remembrance and renewal. Building resilience through grief isn't about developing an impenetrable shield against pain, but rather about nurturing our capacity to weather emotional storms while staying rooted in what matters most. Like tending to a garden, this process requires gentle attention, consistent care, and an understanding that growth happens gradually, often in ways we don't immediately notice.

This truth became beautifully evident where support participants explored resilience through a shared gardening project. The group began with small, manageable tasks planting seeds, daily watering, and gentle tending. One participant initially struggled with the idea of nurturing new growth, feeling it somehow diminished their loss. However, as the weeks progressed, they noticed how the garden's slow, steady development mirrored their own healing journey. Some days, despite careful tending, plants struggled; other days brought unexpected blooms. The process taught valuable lessons about patience, the importance of consistent small actions, and how growth occurs alongside, not in place of grief. The garden became a living metaphor for resilience not as a dramatic transformation, but as a series of small, nurturing steps that gradually built strength while honouring what was lost.

This experience demonstrated how resilience develops through gentle, consistent practices rather than forced 'moving on,' showing how healing can coexist with ongoing grief. It's about finding ways to stand steady even as the ground beneath us shifts, developing new roots while honouring the soil of our experiences. As we explore the concept of resilience in grief, we'll discover practical tools and gentle approaches that help build internal strength while respecting the profound nature of loss.

In this chapter, we'll examine how small, intentional steps can gradually build our capacity to carry grief while moving forward in life. We'll explore specific practices that nurture resilience, from setting compassionate boundaries to developing flexible coping strategies. Most importantly, we'll understand how building resilience honours rather than diminishes our losses, creating space for both remembrance and renewal in our ongoing journey of healing.

Self-Compassion Practices: Building Inner Resources for Healing

At the heart of building resilience through grief lies the essential practice of self-compassion treating ourselves with the same kindness we would offer a dear friend experiencing loss. When grief overwhelms us, we often become our harshest critics, judging our emotions, questioning our coping methods, and pushing ourselves to 'get better' faster. Yet this internal pressure can actually hinder our healing process and deplete the very resources we need to navigate our grief journey.

Self-compassion begins with acknowledging that grief is not a weakness to overcome, but a natural response to loss that deserves gentle attention and care. This might mean giving ourselves permission to rest when fatigue sets in, to cry when emotions surface, or to decline social invitations when we need solitude. These aren't signs of failing at grief they're expressions of honouring our needs during a challenging time.

Consider these foundational practices for building self-compassion:
- Create a daily comfort ritual, such as morning journaling or evening meditation
- Practice gentle self-talk by replacing critical thoughts with understanding ones
- Set realistic expectations for daily tasks, breaking them into manageable steps
- Allow yourself to say 'no' to obligations that feel overwhelming
- Keep a self-compassion journal to track moments of kindness toward yourself

The power of self-compassion lies in its ability to transform our relationship with grief from one of struggle and resistance to one of gentle acceptance and growth. When we meet our pain with kindness rather than judgment, we create space for authentic healing to occur. This doesn't mean the pain disappears, but rather that we develop a more sustainable way of carrying it.

One particularly effective practice involves creating a 'self-compassion pause', a brief moment during challenging times to acknowledge our suffering and respond with kindness. This might involve placing a hand on your heart, taking three deep breaths, and offering yourself words of comfort: 'This is a moment of difficulty. Grief is hard. May I be kind to myself in this moment.'

Building inner resources through self-compassion also means recognising and honouring our limitations. During grief, our capacity for work, social interaction, and even basic tasks may fluctuate dramatically. Rather than pushing through these limitations, self-compassion invites us to respect them as important signals from our body and mind about what we need in the moment.

Consider developing these practical self-compassion strategies:
- Create a 'comfort corner' in your home with soothing items
- Write self-compassionate letters to yourself during difficult moments
- Practice mindful self-touch, like gentle hand massage or face touching
- Keep a list of kind, supportive phrases to reference when grief intensifies

Remember that building self-compassion is itself a practice that requires patience and persistence. Some days it may feel natural and helpful, while others it might seem impossible or inadequate. This too is part of the journey. The goal isn't to perfect self-compassion but to gradually build it into our daily lives as a reliable resource for healing.

Physical self-compassion practices can be particularly grounding during intense grief periods. Simple activities like taking a warm bath, wrapping yourself in a soft blanket, or practicing gentle stretching can help soothe your nervous system and remind your body that it's safe to rest and heal. These physical practices become anchors of kindness we can return to repeatedly throughout our grief journey.

As we cultivate self-compassion, we often discover that it not only supports our grief journey but also helps us maintain connections with our lost loved ones in healthier ways. Rather than feeling guilty about moments of joy or peace, self-compassion helps us understand that healing honours rather than betrays our love for those we've lost. It creates space for both our grief and our growth, allowing us to carry our losses while gradually building resilience for the path ahead.

Adaptive Coping: Developing Flexible

Responses to Grief Triggers

Grief triggers can emerge unexpectedly, catching us off guard and temporarily overwhelming our usual coping mechanisms. Developing adaptive coping strategies means building a flexible toolkit of responses that can be adjusted based on the situation, our energy levels, and our immediate needs. Like a skilled sailor who learns to adjust their sails to different wind conditions, we too can learn to respond to grief triggers with greater adaptability and resilience.

Consider these fundamental aspects of adaptive coping:
- Recognise your personal grief triggers and their patterns
- Develop multiple coping strategies for different situations
- Create emergency comfort measures for intense moments
- Build a support network that understands your needs
- Practice grounding techniques for overwhelming moments

Adaptive coping acknowledges that what works one day might not work the next, and that's perfectly normal. Some days, we might need active coping strategies like exercise or creative expression, while other days might require gentle, passive approaches like quiet reflection or rest. The key is developing awareness of what we need in each moment and having various tools ready to meet those needs.

One effective approach involves creating a 'coping menu', a personalised list of strategies categorised by energy level and situation. For instance, your high energy coping tools might include physical activities or social engagement, while low energy options could include meditation or listening to calming music. Having these options readily available can help you respond more effectively when grief triggers arise.

Consider these situational coping strategies:
- For workplace triggers: Brief breathing exercises, stepping outside, or touching a grounding object
- For social events: Planning exit strategies, bringing a

supportive friend, or taking regular breaks
- For significant dates: Creating new traditions, planning meaningful activities, or seeking extra support
- For unexpected reminders: Carrying comfort items, practicing self-soothing techniques, or using visualisation

Developing flexible responses also means learning to read your own emotional weather patterns. Just as we check the forecast before planning outdoor activities, we can learn to recognise our grief patterns and prepare accordingly. This might mean scheduling additional self-care before anticipated challenging days or arranging support during typically difficult periods.

The practice of adaptive coping extends beyond just managing difficult moments it's about building a sustainable relationship with our grief that can flex and adjust as our needs change. This might involve regularly reassessing our coping strategies, discarding what no longer serves us, and incorporating new tools as we discover them.

Remember these key principles when developing your adaptive coping toolkit:
- Start small and build gradually
- Test new strategies in low stress situations first
- Keep what works and modify what doesn't
- Allow strategies to evolve as your needs change
- Maintain a variety of options for different circumstances

Adaptive coping also involves understanding that setbacks are not failures but opportunities to refine our approach. Each challenging moment provides information about what we need and how we can better support ourselves in the future. This perspective helps transform difficult experiences into stepping stones for growth and healing.

Practical implementation of adaptive coping might look like creating a 'grief first aid kit' a collection of items and reminders that can help during intense moments. This could include comfort objects, written affirmations, grounding exercises, and contact information for key support people. Having these resources readily available can provide a sense of security and preparedness when grief triggers arise.

It's also important to recognise that adaptive coping includes knowing when to seek additional support. Sometimes the most adaptive response is acknowledging when we need help and reaching out to others whether that's friends, family, or professional support. This flexibility in recognising and meeting our needs is itself a powerful coping skill.

As we develop our adaptive coping strategies, we often discover that they not only help us manage grief triggers but also enhance our overall resilience and emotional wellbeing. These skills become valuable tools for navigating life's challenges while honouring our ongoing connection to what we've lost.

Finding Meaning: Creating Purpose Through Loss While Honouring Grief

Finding meaning after loss doesn't mean searching for a silver lining or trying to make sense of the senseless. Instead, it's about discovering ways to honour our grief while gradually building purpose that feels authentic and meaningful. This delicate balance requires patience, self-compassion, and an understanding that meaning often emerges slowly, like dawn breaking after a long night.

Consider these foundational aspects of meaning making through grief:
- Honouring your loss through acts of remembrance
- Creating legacy projects that reflect your loved one's values
- Finding ways to help others experiencing similar journeys
- Transforming grief into meaningful action
- Discovering new purpose while maintaining connections to the past

In a grief support circle, participants explored different ways of creating meaning while honouring their losses. One member found purpose in establishing a community garden where others could come to reflect and remember their loved ones. What began as a simple act of planting flowers in memory of their loss evolved into a healing space that served the broader community while maintaining a deeply personal connection to their grief journey.

The process of finding meaning often begins with small, manageable steps rather than grand gestures. Sometimes it's as simple as carrying forward a loved one's favourite tradition or incorporating their values into our daily lives. These subtle acts of remembrance can gradually build into more substantial ways of creating meaning while honouring our ongoing grief.

It's important to recognise that finding meaning doesn't require extraordinary actions or dramatic transformations. Consider these accessible ways to begin:

- Volunteering with organisations that reflect your loved one's passions
- Starting a memory journal to document stories and reflections
- Creating art or music that expresses your grief journey
- Supporting others who are experiencing similar losses
- Advocating for causes that were important to your loved one

The key is finding activities that feel authentic to your relationship with loss rather than forcing yourself into prescribed roles or actions. Meaning making should never feel like a betrayal of your grief or an attempt to 'replace' what was lost. Instead, it's about finding ways to carry your loss forward while gradually building new purpose.

One particularly powerful approach involves identifying values or qualities that were important to your loved one and finding ways to embody these in your own life. This might mean carrying forward their commitment to education, their love of nature, or their dedication to helping others. By doing so, we create living legacies that honour both our loss and our continued growth.

Remember these essential principles when exploring meaning

making:
- Take small, manageable steps rather than rushing into major changes
- Allow meaning to emerge naturally rather than forcing it
- Honour both your grief and your need for continued purpose
- Remain flexible as your relationship with loss evolves
- Seek support when navigating challenging aspects of this journey

The process of finding meaning through loss often involves periods of questioning and uncertainty. There may be times when purpose feels elusive or when grief seems to overshadow any sense of meaning. These experiences are normal parts of the journey and don't indicate failure or lack of progress.

Creating meaning while honouring grief also involves giving ourselves permission to experience joy without guilt. This might mean celebrating small achievements, embracing new opportunities, or finding moments of peace while maintaining our connection to what was lost. Understanding that joy and grief can coexist helps us build more sustainable approaches to meaning making.

As we explore ways to create purpose through loss, it's crucial to remain gentle with ourselves and patient with the process. Meaning often reveals itself gradually, through small moments of connection and purpose rather than dramatic revelations. This gentle approach allows us to honour both our grief and our need for continued growth, creating space for both remembrance and renewal in our ongoing journey. Building resilience through grief is an ongoing journey that requires patience, self-care, and a willingness to adapt our approach as our needs change. Throughout this chapter, we've explored how small, intentional steps can gradually strengthen our capacity to carry grief while moving forward in life. Like tending to a garden, this process involves consistent care, gentle attention, and an understanding that growth happens in its own time.

The path to resilience isn't about 'getting over' our grief or leaving it behind. Instead, it's about developing tools and practices that help us navigate life while honouring our losses. Through self-care practices, we learn to treat ourselves with the kindness we need during difficult moments. By developing adaptive coping strategies, we build flexibility in responding to grief triggers. And in finding meaning, we discover ways to carry our losses forward while gradually creating purpose that feels authentic and sustainable.

Key elements for building resilience include:
- Practicing self-care and setting gentle boundaries
- Developing flexible coping strategies for different situations
- Creating meaningful rituals and practices that honour loss
- Building supportive connections while respecting personal needs
- Allowing space for both grief and growth

Remember that resilience doesn't mean becoming impervious to pain or never experiencing grief's impact. Rather, it means developing the internal resources to weather emotional storms while staying connected to what matters most. Some days will be harder than others, and that's perfectly normal. What matters is continuing to take small steps forward while being gentle with ourselves along the way.

As we conclude this chapter, consider that building resilience is itself an act of honouring our losses. By learning to carry our grief with greater strength and wisdom, we create space for both remembrance and renewal. This journey may not follow a straight path, but with patience and consistent care, we can gradually build the resilience needed to navigate life after loss while keeping our connections to those we've lost alive in our hearts.

10. THE ONGOING JOURNEY: LIVING MEANINGFULLY WITH LOSS

Living meaningfully with loss isn't about reaching a destination where grief no longer exists, but about learning to carry it with growing wisdom and grace. Like a river that carves new paths while maintaining its essential flow, we too can forge new ways of being while honouring the profound impact of our losses. As we journey through grief, life continues to unfold with its mix of challenges and opportunities, each presenting a unique chance to weave our loss into the tapestry of our evolving story. The path forward isn't about leaving our grief behind, but rather about learning to carry it with growing wisdom while remaining open to new experiences and connections.

In the ebb and flow of daily life, we encounter moments that both honour our past and beckon us toward future possibilities. These transitions can be particularly challenging, as illustrated by a member of a long term grief support group who faced their child's graduation an event that sparked both celebration and profound sadness. Their approach to this milestone demonstrated the delicate balance of honouring absence while embracing presence. By leaving an empty chair adorned with their partner's favourite flower, sharing cherished stories, and creating a photo album that bridged past and present, they found a way to acknowledge both their grief and joy.

This chapter explores how we can create a life that makes space for both our ongoing connection to what we've lost and our continuing growth. We'll examine practical strategies for navigating significant life events, managing the complex emotions that arise during transitions, and finding ways to honour our losses while remaining open to new possibilities. Through understanding how to integrate our grief journey into daily life, we can discover paths forward that feel both authentic and meaningful.

Just as grief transforms over time, so too does our relationship with loss. Rather than seeking closure or an endpoint to our grief, we'll explore how to build a life that acknowledges both the weight of our losses and the potential for continued growth and connection. This journey isn't about reaching a destination where grief no longer exists, but about learning to live fully while carrying our losses with grace and understanding.

Integrating Loss: Building a Life That Honours Both Past and Present

Integrating loss into our lives requires a delicate balance of honouring our past while remaining open to present experiences. This process isn't about compartmentalising grief or relegating it to certain times or places, but rather about finding ways to carry our losses while continuing to engage meaningfully with life. Like a skilled weaver working with different threads, we can learn to intertwine our memories and ongoing connections with new experiences and relationships.

One helpful approach is creating rituals that bridge past and present. These might include:
- Setting aside regular time for remembrance while maintaining daily routines
- Finding ways to include lost loved ones in new traditions
- Creating physical spaces that honour both memories and

current life
- Developing meaningful practices that connect past relationships with present activities

The integration of loss often manifests in unexpected ways throughout our daily lives. A grief support group participant shared how they transformed their Sunday morning routine, which used to revolve around shared coffee and crosswords with their partner. Rather than abandoning this tradition entirely or maintaining it exactly as before, they adapted it. They still do the crossword but now share it with their grandchildren over video chat, teaching them words and creating new memories while honouring the origin of this special time.

It's essential to understand that integrating loss doesn't mean diminishing its significance or 'moving on' from grief. Instead, it's about finding ways to honour our losses while remaining engaged with life's ongoing journey. This might involve:
- Acknowledging significant dates while creating new meaningful occasions
- Sharing stories about lost loved ones while building new relationships
- Maintaining connections to the past while exploring new interests
- Finding ways to channel grief into meaningful activities or causes

The process of integration often requires patience and self-compassion. Some days, the weight of loss might feel heavier than others, and that's perfectly normal. The key is developing flexibility in how we respond to these fluctuations. We might need different approaches for different situations sometimes actively incorporating our loss into current experiences, other times simply acknowledging its presence while focusing on present moments.

One particularly effective strategy for integration involves finding ways to honour our losses through actions that benefit others or contribute to causes that feel meaningful.

This might include:
- Volunteering for organisations connected to our loss
- Sharing our experience to help others facing similar challenges
- Creating projects or initiatives that honour what we've lost
- Finding ways to continue the values or legacy of what we've lost

As we work to integrate our losses, it's important to remember that this isn't a linear process with a clear endpoint. Some days we might feel more connected to our grief, while others might bring more engagement with present experiences. Both are valid and natural parts of living with loss. The goal isn't to 'solve' grief but to learn to carry it while remaining open to life's continuing journey.

Creating a life that honours both past and present also involves giving ourselves permission to experience joy without guilt. This might mean:
- Acknowledging that new happiness doesn't diminish past relationships
- Understanding that laughter and tears can coexist
- Recognising that growth honours rather than betrays what we've lost
- Accepting that our capacity for love and connection can expand rather than replace

Through mindful integration, we can build lives that honour our losses while remaining open to new experiences and connections. This balance allows us to carry our grief not as a burden that holds us back, but as a profound part of who we are, informing and enriching our ongoing journey through life.

Navigating Milestones: Managing Grief Through Life's Transitions

Life's milestones and transitions can intensify grief in unexpected ways, often catching us off guard with their emotional complexity. Whether it's birthdays, anniversaries, graduations, or other significant life events, these moments can bring both celebration and sorrow, requiring thoughtful navigation and gentle self-care. Understanding how to approach these transitions while honouring our grief can help us move through them with greater ease and authenticity.

- Milestones often trigger a complex mix of emotions that can feel overwhelming. Common reactions include:
- Heightened awareness of absence during traditionally shared celebrations
- Unexpected waves of grief during otherwise joyful occasions
- Difficulty participating in events that highlight life's continuing forward motion
- Conflicting feelings of guilt and joy when experiencing positive moments

Navigating these transitions requires preparation and self-awareness. Creating a flexible approach to handling significant events can help manage their emotional impact while honouring both our grief and the importance of these moments.

Consider developing a 'milestone toolkit' that might include:
- Specific strategies for managing overwhelming emotions during events
- Plans for incorporating remembrance into celebrations
- Support systems to call upon during challenging transitions
- Permission to adjust or limit participation as needed

One support group participant shared their approach to managing their wedding anniversary after loss. Rather than trying to ignore the date or becoming overwhelmed by grief, they created a new tradition that honoured both their loss and their continuing life journey. Each year, they spend part of the day in quiet reflection and remembrance, then engage in an activity that represents growth or learning something their partner would have appreciated but they'd never done together. This approach exemplifies how we can acknowledge our grief while still moving forward with life.

When facing significant transitions, it's helpful to prepare by:
- Anticipating emotional triggers and planning appropriate responses
- Communicating needs and boundaries to friends and family
- Creating space for both celebration and remembrance
- Allowing flexibility in how we participate in events

The workplace often presents its own set of milestone challenges, from company anniversaries to team celebrations. Developing strategies for managing these professional transitions while honouring our grief is essential. This might include:
- Having honest conversations with supervisors about challenging dates
- Creating modified ways to participate in team events
- Establishing private moments for processing emotions during workdays
- Setting clear boundaries around participation in social activities

It's important to remember that our response to milestones may change over time. What feels impossible one year might feel manageable the next, and vice versa. This fluctuation is normal and deserves our patience and understanding. We might need different approaches for different events or different phases of our grief journey.

When supporting others through milestone transitions, consider:
- Acknowledging both the celebration and the difficulty of the moment
- Offering specific, practical support rather than general statements
- Following their lead on how much they want to participate or discuss
- Respecting their need to modify traditions or create new

ones

Navigating milestones also involves managing others' expectations and potential misunderstandings. Some people might not understand why certain events remain challenging even years after a loss. Creating clear communication strategies can help:
- Express needs and boundaries clearly and directly
- Share plans for managing events in advance
- Identify specific ways others can provide support
- Maintain the right to modify or decline participation as needed

Through mindful preparation and self-compassion, we can learn to navigate life's transitions while honouring our grief. This doesn't mean these moments will be easy, but with proper support and understanding, we can find ways to acknowledge both our losses and life's continuing journey. Remember that each milestone navigated is an achievement, regardless of how we choose to approach it.

Creating Legacy: Finding Purpose Through Loss While Maintaining Connection

Finding purpose through loss while maintaining meaningful connections to what we've lost can become a powerful part of our healing journey. This process isn't about replacing or diminishing our grief, but rather about channelling it into actions and initiatives that honour both our loss and our continuing life journey. Creating legacy allows us to transform our grief into meaningful impact while strengthening our ongoing connection to what we've lost.

One of the most healing aspects of creating legacy involves finding ways to continue the values, passions, or causes that were important to what we've lost. This might include:
- Supporting organisations or causes that held special meaning
- Continuing traditions or practices that embody important

values
- Creating new initiatives that extend the impact of what mattered most
- Finding ways to share wisdom or lessons learned through our loss

A grief support group participant shared how they transformed their grief into purpose by establishing a community garden project. Their loved one had been passionate about bringing people together and nurturing growth. The garden became not just a memorial, but a living legacy that continued these values, providing a space for community connection while honouring their loved one's impact on others.

Creating legacy can take many forms, and it's important to find approaches that feel authentic to our experience and energy levels. Some meaningful ways to create legacy include:
- Establishing scholarship or education funds
- Volunteering for relevant organisations
- Creating art or writing that expresses our experience
- Mentoring others facing similar challenges

However, it's crucial to remember that legacy building should come from a place of readiness rather than obligation. Forcing ourselves into legacy projects before we're emotionally prepared can complicate our grief journey. Instead, allow these initiatives to develop naturally as part of our healing process.

Maintaining connection while creating legacy involves finding balance between honouring what was lost and embracing new purpose. This might mean:
- Incorporating elements of our loss into new projects or initiatives
- Finding ways to share stories and memories through our legacy work
- Creating spaces that honour both remembrance and forward movement
- Allowing our grief to inform but not overwhelm our

purpose

One particularly effective approach involves creating legacy projects that benefit others while maintaining personal meaning. This dual purpose can help us:
- Transform pain into purposeful action
- Build supportive communities around shared experiences
- Create ongoing opportunities for remembrance
- Find meaning through helping others

It's important to recognise that legacy creation isn't about achieving specific outcomes or meeting others' expectations. Instead, it's about finding ways to honour our loss that feel meaningful and sustainable for us. This might mean starting small and allowing our initiatives to grow naturally over time.

When developing legacy projects, consider:
- Starting with manageable goals that respect your energy levels
- Allowing flexibility in how projects evolve
- Creating space for both active work and quiet reflection
- Building in ways to adjust or step back when needed

Maintaining connection through legacy work also involves finding ways to include others who shared our loss. This collaborative approach can:
- Strengthen existing relationships through shared purpose
- Create new connections with others who understand our experience
- Provide mutual support through meaningful action
- Expand the impact of our legacy initiatives

As we create legacy, it's essential to maintain healthy boundaries and self-care practices. Legacy work shouldn't become another source of pressure or obligation in our grief journey. Instead, it should provide a meaningful way to honour our loss while contributing to our healing process.

Remember that creating legacy is an ongoing journey rather

than a destination. Our projects and initiatives may evolve as our relationship with grief changes over time. This evolution is natural and allows our legacy work to remain authentic and meaningful as we continue our healing journey. As we conclude this exploration of living meaningfully with loss, it becomes clear that our grief journey doesn't end but rather evolves, becoming an integral part of who we are and how we move through the world. Like the gradual changing of seasons, our relationship with grief shifts and transforms while maintaining its essential presence in our lives.

The stories and experiences shared throughout this chapter remind us that integrating loss into our ongoing life journey requires both patience and intention. Whether navigating professional spaces, celebrating milestones, or creating meaningful legacies, we've seen how it's possible to honour our grief while remaining open to new experiences and connections. This balance isn't about diminishing our loss but about expanding our capacity to carry it with growing wisdom and grace.

Key insights that emerge from our exploration include:
- The importance of creating flexible approaches to managing grief in different life contexts
- The value of establishing meaningful rituals that bridge past and present
- The power of finding purpose through loss while maintaining authentic connections
- The necessity of setting boundaries and managing expectations during significant transitions

As you continue your unique journey with grief, remember that each step forward doesn't mean leaving your loss behind, but rather learning to carry it in ways that feel authentic and meaningful to you. Your path may look different from others, and that's not just okay it's exactly as it should be.

The tools and strategies we've explored aren't meant to 'fix' your grief but to help you navigate it with greater understanding and self-compassion. Whether you're facing workplace challenges, approaching significant milestones, or seeking ways to create meaningful legacy, remember that you have the right to move at your own pace and in your own way.

Perhaps most importantly, this chapter reminds us that living meaningfully with loss isn't about reaching a destination where grief no longer exists. Instead, it's about learning to weave our loss into the fabric of our lives in ways that honour both our past connections and our continuing journey. As you move forward, carry with you the understanding that grief and growth can coexist, that joy and sorrow can share space in your heart, and that finding new meaning doesn't diminish the significance of what you've lost.

Your grief journey continues beyond these pages, unique and personal to you. May you find comfort in knowing that while the path forward may not always be clear, you have the strength and wisdom within you to navigate it in ways that feel true to your experience. Remember that living meaningfully with loss isn't about getting it 'right', it's about finding your way forward while honouring the profound impact of your loss.

CONCLUSION

Throughout this journey of exploring grief and loss, we've navigated the varied landscapes of human experience, acknowledging that each person's path through grief is as unique as their fingerprint. The stories and insights shared in these pages reflect the universal truth that grief, in all its forms, deserves validation, understanding, and gentle support.

We've examined how grief manifests in countless ways, from the profound loss of loved ones to the quieter grief of lost dreams and identities. We've explored how our bodies speak the language of loss, how professional spaces can accommodate healing, and how creating sacred spaces for mourning can anchor us in turbulent times. Through each chapter, we've reinforced that there is no timeline for grief, no 'right way' to mourn, and no requirement to 'move on' according to others' expectations.

The tools, strategies, and insights offered here are not meant to fix or erase your grief, but rather to help you carry it with growing wisdom and grace. Remember that building resilience doesn't mean leaving your grief behind it means developing the strength to hold both your loss and your hope for the future. As you continue on your journey, know that your grief is a reflection of love, and your way of honouring it is valid and worthy of respect.

The fog of grief may remain, shifting and changing like weather patterns, but you now have tools to navigate through it. You understand that mindful mourning, compassionate self-care, and meaningful remembrance can light the way forward. You've learned that building a supportive environment, whether at home or work, can create space for both grieving and growing.

As you close these pages, remember that this book is not an endpoint but a companion on your ongoing journey. The insights and practices shared here can be revisited whenever you need them, offering fresh perspective and renewed support as your relationship with grief evolves. You may find different sections resonate more strongly at different times, this too is part of grief's fluid nature.

Your capacity to carry grief while building a meaningful life is stronger than you might imagine. Through the stories shared and lessons explored, you've seen how others have navigated similar waters, finding ways to honour their losses while gradually opening to new possibilities. Your journey may follow a different course, but you now have a compass to help guide your way.

Moving forward doesn't mean leaving behind what you've lost but rather learning to weave your loss into the tapestry of your life with tenderness and intention. The connections you cherish, the memories you hold dear, and the love you carry remain vital parts of your story. As you continue on your path, may you find comfort in knowing that your grief is acknowledged, your journey is respected, and your healing, however it unfolds, is valid.

Remember that support remains available long after these pages end. Whether through professional counselling, support groups, or compassionate friends who understand grief's enduring nature, you don't have to walk this path alone. Your grief may change shape over time, but it need not be silenced or rushed. Take what serves you from these pages, trust your instincts, and know that wherever your journey leads, your authentic way of grieving is worthy of honour and respect.

Reference

Attig, T. (2010). How We Grieve: Relearning the World. Oxford University Press.

Bosticco, C., & Thompson, T. L. (2005). Narratives and story telling in coping with grief and bereavement. OMEGA Journal of Death and Dying, 51(1), 1 16.

Doka, K. J. (2002). Disenfranchised Grief: New Directions, Challenges, and Strategies for Practice. Research Press.

Kübler Ross, E., & Kessler, D. (2005). On Grief and Grieving: Finding the Meaning of Grief Through the Five Stages of Loss. Simon & Schuster.

Neimeyer, R. A. (2012). Techniques of Grief Therapy: Creative Practices for Counseling the Bereaved. Routledge.

Prigerson, H. G., & Maciejewski, P. K. (2008). Grief and acceptance as opposite sides of the same coin: setting a research agenda to study peaceful acceptance of loss. The British Journal of Psychiatry, 193(6), 435 437.

Stroebe, M., & Schut, H. (1999). The dual process model of coping with bereavement: Rationale and description. Death Studies, 23(3), 197 224.

Worden, J. W. (2018). Grief Counseling and Grief Therapy: A Handbook for the Mental Health Practitioner (5th ed.). Springer Publishing Company.

Dream About Falling Off Cliff Betrayed By Dad. https://dreamapp.io/common dreams/im on the edge of a cliff

Soulful Rituals: Infusing Spirituality Into Daily Life. https://theenlightenmentjourney.com/soulful rituals infusing spirituality into daily life/

ABOUT THE AUTHOR

Debbie Bryden

After experiencing profound loss and navigating my own journey through grief, my commitment to breaking the silence around grief and creating safe spaces for authentic grieving experiences stems from my own transformation of deep loss into purposeful connection with others walking similar paths. With decades of managing teams and customers through grief vulnerability, and with professional training, I have drawn on these experiences to guide and support others identify grieving behaviours and help them to navigate a coping strategy.

Printed in Great Britain
by Amazon